"Full of great wisdom, perspectives and "to do's" on building, running and growing a great business."

—David Pottruck, President and Co-CEO, Charles Schwab Corporation

"The best in business for those who want to go beyond survival."

—John Caple, author of *Trust Me*

Zebras Don't Wear Pinstripes

The Business Jungle

Sales Success Series

by

Thomas T. Brown

Remember the Big Picture
and you will prosper!

PUBLISHER'S NOTE

This publication is designed to provide accurate and authoritative information in regard to the subject matter covered. It is sold with the understanding that the publisher is not engaged in rendering marketing, management or other professional service. If professional advice or other expert assistance is required, the service of a competent professional person should be sought.

Cypress Publishing Group, Inc.
1835 Roe # 187
Leawood, KS 66211
www.cypresspublishing.com

Library of Congress Cataloging-in-Publication Data

Brown, Thomas T.
    Zebras Don't Wear Pinstripes/ by Tom T. Brown
    Includes index.
        p. cm.
    ISBN: 0-89447-324-7
    1.   2.   I. Title.

Printed in the United States of America

10 9 8 7 6 5 4 3 2 1

Dedication

To Bob and Shar Rubin, who made the first safari possible, I say *Asante sana.*

To Francy and Troy, for joining me on the biggest safari of all, I say *I love you.*

Acknowledgments

To the "Editorial Board:" John and Kathy Conley, Leslie Jo Filson, Lyn Haston, Rick Haenggi for giving me your time.

To Ted Rose for giving me the luxury of automation.

To Catherine Munson for giving me the seeds of my network.

To my "Master Minds:" John Caple, Jay Levinson, Terry Pearce for sharing their advice and encouragement.

Thank you everyone, look what we've created.

Table of Contents

Preface

This is a book about improving your business. Although the book takes place in a mythical east African country, and although a major character is a native tribal woman, this is not a book about Africa, its culture or its people. I am not an anthropologist.

This book describes the *real* laws of the *real* jungle and tells how those laws can be adapted to the world of business. In the following pages much is written about animal behavior, but this is not a book about wildlife biology or ecology. I am not a scientist.

I have spent time in eastern Africa and have successfully completed my own photo safari during which I photographed the Big Five game animals (cheetah, lion, rhino, Cape buffalo and elephant). I have met members of the great native tribes. However, I do not presume to be an expert about the people or animals of Africa, and all the characters in this book are fictional.

It has been my good fortune to work with and for many fine people during my professional career (both men and women). Being a success in business has nothing to do with gender. It has everything to do with integrity, passion, intelligence and commitment. These qualities are not masculine or feminine; they are human. In writing this book, I chose to avoid employing the traditional use of entirely male nouns and pronouns because it just doesn't feel right. Instead I have used both masculine and feminine nouns and pronouns.

The Laws of the Jungle presented in The Business Jungle Books apply to all types of enterprises: retail, wholesale, manufacturing, professional, personal service, and more. But the people who do business with these enterprises have different labels; some are labeled *customers* and some are labeled *clients*. For example retail stores have *customers,* but professionals have *clients*. What's the difference?

Customers are people with whom transactions take place. If you walk into a grocery store to buy eggs, milk and butter, then you're a *customer*. The grocery store's objective is to do a lot of transactions with you.

Clients are people for whom professional services are provided. If you visit your attorney to discuss your estate plan and get a new will, then you're a *client*. The attorney's objective is to have a relationship with you that transcends the business you transact.

In order to recognize the spectrum of businesses to which the Laws of the Jungle apply I have also alternated the use of the terms *customer* and *client* between chapters.

You will find both Business Jungle Survival *Tools* and Business Jungle Survival *Skills* throughout the book. Both of these sales productivity aids will make you a better salesperson. Both will address a wide range of sales skills and offer solutions to the challenges you face each day.

Business Jungle Survival T*ools* are worksheets, planning documents and other sales productivity aids that are implementation tools. They are activities that you can perform. They involve you in answering questions by writing down ideas and filling in the blanks. Feel free to make copies of them so you can use them without writing in your book.

Business Jungle Survival *Skills* are something else. They are suggested strategies that you can implement on your own. They are behaviors you can adopt. They engage you by asking you to think about techniques, policies and procedures.

Now, come with me into the Jungle...

Map of the Masara Masai
and
the route of the Salesman's safari

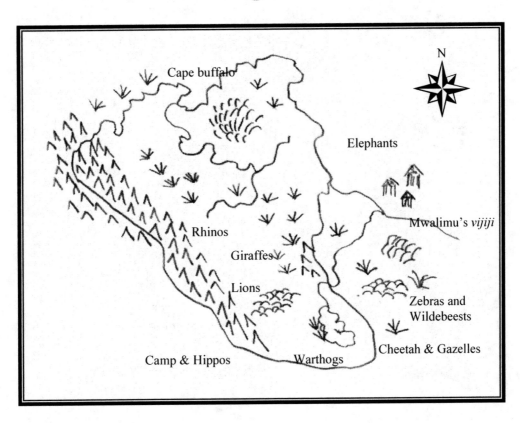

Now these are the Laws of the Jungle, and many and mighty are they;
But the head and the hoof of the Law and the haunch and the hump is— Obey!

—Rudyard Kipling, *The Jungle Books*

Chapter One

THE TEACHER

"So, what brings you to Tanganda?" inquired the driver of the Land Rover.

The Salesman sighed before he replied. "It's been a long time since I took a vacation, and I really needed to get as far away from the office as possible so that I can do something to get my mind off of business."

"Well, you picked the right place. Here in Tanganda you can learn about *hakuna matata*. It took a children's cartoon to tell the world about *hakuna matata*, but we have believed this philosophy for a very long time. It is part of our culture. It essentially means: your days will have no troubles," said the driver cheerfully.

The Salesman had to agree with the driver, Tanganda did seem to be the right place. He had logged almost 20 hours of exhausting, uncomfortable and sometimes white-knuckled flight time to finally arrive here in the Masara Masai region of Tanganda near the border with Tanzania. That, he thought, certainly had to qualify as "far away." As a matter of fact, there probably weren't too many other places on earth any farther away from his office.

This diversion was really a necessity. In fact he was counting on this trip to recharge his batteries and somehow infuse him with the energy he needed, but couldn't seem to muster, to help him climb off the professional plateau he had reached.

The Salesman had spent most of his professional career selling investment products and advising clients on investing their money. He had become quite good at his profession. He had studied for and received numerous professional designations and certifications. He had acquired more and more clients, and his business steadily grew. He had even won countless sales contests and received prestigious awards from his employer. Now he was stuck. He'd hit the wall. He had reached a professional plateau and couldn't figure out how to climb to the next level of success.

The Salesman was very frustrated by his professional predicament. Success had spoiled him. He was used to setting and achieving difficult goals. Frankly, he was used to getting what he wanted. What he wanted now was to increase his annual production by at least 20%. It was a challenging but attainable goal and one that he had achieved in past years. But lately his production had remained stubbornly level, or even slightly below prior years. He was doing the same things that had helped him achieve his production goals in previous years, but the results weren't the same. This is what made him so terribly frustrated.

One day a colleague told him: "It's obvious that you're *not* doing the same things you've always done. If you were, you would be well on the way to the next level of success. Here's what I think you ought to do: Have a meeting with yourself. In that meeting ask yourself if you're *really* doing the things you used to do, or do you just *think* you are. Maybe you've forgotten some of the fundamentals of your prior success. Did you know that when Vince Lombardi took over as head coach of the Green Bay Packers, he believed that the team needed to focus on fundamentals to be a winner? He got his team to refocus on fundamentals by starting off his first team meeting by holding a football up and saying, 'Gentlemen, this is a football.' Maybe you've just forgotten what the football looks like. And have you considered this? Maybe the things you used to do simply don't work today. Maybe you need to try some new things, too. But the very first thing you need to do is take some time off. You're too close to the problem. Take a step back. Take your mind off of it for a while. Do yourself a favor; take a vacation!"

…And so here he was. Rattling across the oatgrass covered savannah of the Masara Masai in a four-wheel drive Land Rover.

"We are very close to the native *vijiji*," announced the driver.

The Salesman had arranged to take a trip to this *vijiji*, the native word for village, with the Safari Club so that he could learn more about the native people.

"Have you ever been to a *vijiji*?" he asked.

"No," replied the Salesman. "This is my first time in Tanganda."

"Most of them look the same," explained the driver. "They're a simple circle of mud huts inside a fence made of thorns. During the day the inner circle is the *vijiji*'s common area. The children play there; the people socialize. A lot of activity happens there. The native people are herders. Early in the morning, the men and young boys take the cattle herds out onto the plains so that they can graze on the grass. At night the cattle stay inside the circle and the thorn bushes keep out the predators. When we get there I will introduce you to Mwalimu, the head woman of this *vijiji*. She is very smart."

"Whatever..." shrugged the Salesman.

"So what kind of a business do you have that you need to get away from?" inquired the driver.

"I'm in the investment business. I'm a stockbroker."

"Wow, that's a good job. I hear that stockbrokers can make a lot of money in the USA."

"I suppose that depends on your definition of *a lot*," said the Salesman curtly.

"Hey, you can tell me if I'm being too nosey," the driver said cheerfully. "But it sounds like you have a good job. How come you need to get so far away and take your mind off of it?"

There was something about the driver's infectious disposition that the Salesman found pleasant. "I just need to figure out some better ways to do business. Sometimes you need to get away and *not* think about a problem in order to solve it."

"So it sounds like you'd like to learn about new ways to do business?" asked the driver.

"I'm always looking for ways to learn more."

"Well, then you should find this *vijiji* very interesting, maybe even fascinating!" the driver said enthusiastically. "The people who live there are the wealthiest natives in the whole region, and Mwalimu is the reason. Mwalimu can tell you all about making *donge*—that's the native word for money."

The Land Rover bounced to a halt in a cloud of dust outside a circle of mud huts. The driver jumped out of the vehicle and was greeted by a half-dozen tall, slender native women. They were elegant people. Their coal-black, glowing skin was offset by the vibrant colors they wore. Most of the women had shaved heads. Those that had any hair at all kept it cut very short. This was so they could show off their equally brilliant earrings and necklaces.

The Salesman wandered off to explore the *vijiji*, hoping to avoid meeting this Mwalimu person. Many of the women were busy working on numerous crafts: jewelry-making, sewing, sandal-making, basket-weaving and carving. He was getting ready to photograph a woman who was painting a carved wooden mask when a voice from behind him said, "I am told that you want to learn more about business from Mwalimu."

The Salesman turned to face a woman who was slightly shorter than the others and appeared to be older. Her age was difficult to determine; she could have been anywhere from 50 to 70.

"Well no, I'm really not looking for any business lessons here. I was just telling the driver on the way out here that I needed to figure out some better ways to do business. He said that someone named Mwalimu, who lived here, had made this *vijiji* very rich and that I could learn something from her. The driver was just being nice, I think he was just trying to make me feel better."

"I am Mwalimu."

Like the other women he had seen, Mwalimu's skin was the color of dark-roasted coffee inside a black ceramic mug. The African sun glinted off her skin as if it were light reflecting off the surface of that coffee. She wore a simple sleeveless dress, called a *kanzu*, which covered her from neck to below her knees. The *kanzu* was fashioned from cotton material in a bold brick red color and bore large geometric designs in green, orange, black, white and blue.

It occurred to the Salesman that he was staring at her and that he ought to introduce himself. "I'm sorry, it's just that you took me by surprise. It's nice to meet you, my name's..."

"I know," she interrupted. "You are the Salesman."

"Yeah, I guess I am. I'm kind of surprised that you speak English."

"One must learn to communicate in ways that will help achieve what one seeks. Speaking English has helped me find what I seek. The driver says you want to learn about business from me. What makes you think I can teach you anything about business? After all, I'm just an old woman living in a mud hut in the middle of nowhere."

Whoa, a mind reader, too, thought the Salesman. "Well now that you ask, I'm not sure that you can."

"Hmmf," she snorted, "*Kikulacho kinguoni mwako.*"

"I don't speak your language, I don't understand what you just said."

"I said that 'you don't have to look beyond yourself to find the source of your problems.' It's a proverb."

"Thanks for the native wisdom. Look, I'm sure you're probably a good teacher. I just don't think you can help me," he replied.

"*Asante sana.* Thank you for the compliment. Yes, I am a very good teacher. You see, in Swahili my name, Mwalimu, means the teacher.*"

"So, Mwalimu. The driver says that you made this *vijuju* rich."

"You mean *vijiji,*" she corrected him. "And, no, I didn't make this *vijiji* rich. I simply recognized an opportunity that no other person in this, or any other nearby *vijiji*, had recognized first. When we understood the power of this venture, we could see that it would make us wealthier than our neighbors. We pursued it and it has brought us much success. Our income is ten times greater than any other *vijiji* in the Masara Masai region."

Mwalimu now had the Salesman's complete attention. "Ten times!? That's impressive. But I'm still not sure that you can tell me much that would help me in my business. I'm an investment broker for crying out loud. Even if you did figure out some way to make your *vijiji* more prosperous, I doubt your methods would apply to the American business world."

"Then you won't be interested in learning more when I tell you that the opportunity I recognized was based upon forming a strategic alliance between two business enterprises. These enterprises were very different, but I thought they could potentially complement each other. I recognized a synergy that no one else had seen. The strategic alliance was negotiated and I was proven right."

Mwalimu continued, "You're staying at the Masara Safari Club, correct? It's a beautiful resort. It's world famous you know. The Masara Safari Club caters to visitors from all over the world. Just like you, many of these guests are interested in learning more about the native people and culture, *my* people and *my* culture. The Club has the enviable reputation of always going out of its way to meet its guest's expectations. But they had no way to provide a true native experience for them. On the other hand, because my *vijiji* is real, it is a true and authentic representation of the way the native people live. As you know, it's quite a trek all the way out here. Although my people are famous for traveling long distances on foot, we knew we couldn't expect a white man to walk all the way to our village."

The Salesman nodded knowingly. "I think I see where this is headed," he interjected.

"Perhaps you do. One day I walked from my *vijiji* to the Club and I spoke to the manager. I told him that I knew he wanted to offer his guests a way to better understand the native culture, but he didn't have the means to do it. Then I told him that my *vijiji* would welcome any of his guests and be proud to tell them about our customs. Alas, we had no way to transport his guests to the *vijiji*. The manager and I talked about the ways we could help one another. I told him our proverb that states that a house without guests is not blessed and that we would take his guests inside our homes. We would tell them about our culture, show them our handicrafts, sing and dance for them, and answer their questions. He told me that this was exactly the kind of experience he was looking to provide for his guests, and he said that his drivers would bring his guests to our *vijiji* in the Club's Land Rovers. We agreed that we would charge the guests a fair price for providing them with this experience and that the Club and the *vijiji* would split the income. In addition, the *vijiji* would keep all of the income from selling our handicrafts. For many years, we have been blessed to greet the guests brought to our homes. We have earned a lot of *donge* from our share of the fees and even more from selling our arts and crafts. Even you have contributed to our prosperity."

"I've got to admit it Mwalimu, you were very resourceful when you recognized the opportunity and capitalized on it. And you're right; you formed a classic strategic business alliance. Each of the two enterprises had a unique service that would complement the other. Each of you had a similar challenge to delivering your service. When the two of you formed your alliance, your combined service could be successfully delivered to a market that neither of you could reach alone. Both of you accomplished your goals, and both of you were able to profit from the alliance. That's a beautiful thing," he said with a note of approval and admiration in his voice.

"So now you see that 'native-style business' as you called it might have relevance to business in the USA after all? Maybe there are some more lessons that you can learn here?" asked Mwalimu.

"Well, I can definitely relate to the story you just told me."

Just before he left on his trip, the financial news was full of reports about giant, multi-billion-dollar mergers and other assorted conglomerates among corporate behemoths. During the previous year, Wall Street had experienced a record volume of such mega-deals. The staggering size of these huge contracts was beyond the Salesman's comprehension. As he was listening to Mwalimu tell her story about the alliance between her *vijiji* and the resort, he was thinking of similar smaller strategic alliances and joint ventures that he too could comprehend. For example, one of the Salesman's clients owned a family-run pizza business. The business was well established and profitable, but competition was getting very tough from a proliferation of local franchises of national pizza chains. The client was trying to figure out a way to creatively increase his business in the face of the competition. He contacted the owner of a local video rental store about putting a pizza counter in his store and also renting the store's videos from a special counter in the pizza restaurant. This way both enterprises could offer the convenience of pizza and a video in one spot. They agreed to try the concept, and it had exceeded their expectations.

The sound of Mwalimu's voice interrupted his train of thought. "Is there a lesson in my story that can help your business? I believe that there probably is," she said with a faint smile on her lips.

"Well, now that you mention it, your story has given me an idea that I might want to try when I get back home," answered the Salesman.

It occurred to him that he might want to form some strategic alliances, too. The Salesman was an expert in equity investments like stocks and mutual funds. But he never really liked to deal with fixed-income investments like Treasury Bills and corporate bonds so he didn't do much business in them. He knew that fixed-income investments were an important part of his clients' portfolios, and he knew there was a large demand for them. He also knew that there was another broker in his firm who specialized in this type of investment. Perhaps he could form an alliance with the other broker. He could refer his clients to the other broker for assistance with fixed income investments and that broker could refer clients to him for assistance with equity investments. Both of them could then focus on what they liked and knew best. They would both undoubtedly do more business, and they could split the commissions they earned from the referred clients. It would be a beautiful thing.

While he was considering this, he remembered that he had already formed some alliances but had let them fade away. He used to spend a lot of time cultivating CPA's, attorneys and other centers of influence that could refer business to him. He hadn't spoken to those referral sources in a long time. Worse yet, he had sometimes forgotten to thank them when they did send a referral. He would have to mend those fences quickly because referred clients were often the best ones.

These were two leads he would be sure to pursue as soon as he got back to his office. If he were successfully able to implement just these two ideas they could take a big bite out of the 20% goal he had set. He was amazed that he had only been talking to Mwalimu for a short time and had already come up with a couple of great business development ideas that had a lot of potential. Most amazing of all was that he wouldn't have thought of them if he hadn't been standing in a circle of mud huts talking to an old native woman.

"Yes, Mwalimu. I'm definitely going to try these ideas. Thank you. I mean, *Asante sana.*"

"*Karibu*, Mwanfunzi, my student. You're welcome. Please tell me what you learned."

"Well," he began, "I think the lesson here has to do with partnering. It's important to be open to forming alliances with other people and organizations. Recognize that other businesses have a challenge that you might help them solve or that other businesses have a solution to a problem that you might have. Together you may be able to reach markets that neither of you could reach alone. The partnership makes you both stronger than you were separately."

"Very perceptive. I think you're getting the hang of observing what happens here in the real jungle and then recognizing lessons that can help you succeed and prosper in the Business Jungle," smiled Mwalimu.

"Earlier you said I was resourceful," she continued. "The trait of resourcefulness is an important one for my people. It is one of our Three R's: respect, responsibility, and resourcefulness," explained Mwalimu.

She swept her arm in front of her. "We respect this beautiful, bountiful land we live on. We respect the wild animals that we live with and who allow us to share this land. We respect the domestic animals that provide us with meat to eat, milk to drink and hides to craft. And we respect the people we encounter every day. We are responsible for our actions. In other words, we do what we say we will do, and we do it when we say we will do it. We try very hard to live up to this responsibility, but if we fail then we readily accept the blame and the consequences of our failure."

"And I recognized your resourcefulness, the last of your Three R's," said the Salesman. He truly was impressed.

"Yes. We feel that this trait is more important than intelligence. Resourcefulness is the ability to apply your intelligence to find a solution to a challenge when no solution is apparent. What good is intelligence if you can't use it to find a solution to a problem? It is true that a person can become more intelligent by studying longer and harder. But becoming resourceful is much more difficult. You can't study it in a book, memorize a formula and pass a test. There is no formula for creativity. Learning to be resourceful is a by-product of the environment in which we live. It is a quality that is acquired as the result of the sum total of a person's experiences. We prize it highly.

"These Three R's of yours make a lot of sense to me," said the Salesman nodding his head. "I can see how these Three R's will change my approach to business."

"Tell me how," she requested.

"Sometimes I take my clients and co-workers for granted. I should show them more respect. Sometimes I try to shift blame when something doesn't go right. I need to assume responsibility for these things. My clients know that no one is perfect; we're all only human, and we all make mistakes. When I assume responsibility by taking ownership, then I will be accountable for fixing a problem when something doesn't go right. By becoming a problem-solver, I'll be more valuable to my clients. Whenever I come up against a challenge that doesn't seem to have an answer I'll remember your lesson about resourcefulness."

After a moment he added, " I guess that native-style business really does have some relevance to American-style business after all. You've opened my eyes, Mwalimu."

"That is the most any teacher can hope to do. Come back tomorrow and you will learn a lesson from the zebra."

The Laws of the Business Jungle

1. **Partnering: Good partnerships make you stronger together than you were separately**.

Your business may be able to solve sales and marketing challenges for other businesses, and other businesses may be able to solve challenges you are facing. If you work together you may be able to reach markets that neither of you could reach alone.

2. **The new Three R's: respect, responsibility and resourcefulness**

Respect the people you do business with, the people you work with, and most of all respect yourself. Show your responsibility by doing what you say you will, and doing it when you say you will do it. Don't shift responsibility. Accept accountability. Resourcefulness is the creative application of your intelligence and experience to find a solution when none seems apparent.

Chapter Two

ZEBRAS DON'T WEAR PINSTRIPES

The Salesman arrived at Mwalimu's *vijiji* in the Safari Club's Land Rover at sunrise the next day.

"*Jambo*, Mwanfunzi. I'm delighted you've come back for another lesson!" she said. "I'm glad you didn't change your mind. Today we will begin with a lesson from the zebra. In my culture, we believe that telling stories is important for learning. That's how we pass along our traditions and our history from one generation to the next. But we also believe that an important part of learning is observation, not merely listening. Yes, I am going to tell you about the zebra, but I also want you to observe the zebra as well."

"I've already seen some zebras. We passed some in the Land Rover on the way back to the Club yesterday. They just look like a bunch of striped horses," the Salesman said impatiently.

"You may have *seen* a herd of zebras, but you hardly *observed* them. Think about it this way. When you view a tropical fish from the outside of its fishbowl, you've merely *seen* it. When you swim over the coral reef in which it lives and view a tropical fish in its natural surroundings, then you have truly *observed* it."

"All right, but how am I supposed to observe the zebras any better than what I saw from the Land Rover? I don't see any zebras around here, and I'm hardly going to go trotting off over the plains looking for them."

"Why not?" asked Mwalimu.

"Why not what?"

"Why not go out on the plains and look for them?"

"Well for one thing it's not legal. For another, I don't want to end up as the main course on some lion's lunch menu."

"You're right," agreed Mwalimu. "It is illegal for you to be out on the plains alone. But you won't be alone; you'll be with me. As far as being on the lion's lunch menu, you don't have to worry about that either. When Simba sees one of my people walking on the savannah he will take off in the opposite direction.

"Let me tell you a short story. In my culture when a boy is about 14 years old, he undertakes a rite of passage in which he leaves boyhood behind and transforms himself into a warrior. As part of his rite of passage he will go on long safaris by himself. He must learn to rely on himself. He must learn to use his wits and his resourcefulness to survive. He must come to terms with the land and the animals and, in so doing, he learns to respect them both, and he also learns to respect himself. I am offering you the chance to experience your own rite of passage. Together we'll go on a safari. We will see many animals, and you will learn many lessons from them that will help you survive in the Business Jungle."

A half-hour later the Salesman and Mwalimu walked eastward out of the *vijiji* into the rising sun and onto the vast plains of the Masara Masai. Against the coolness of the early morning air Mwalimu wore a woolen blanket over her shawl that would also serve as her bedroll. Under the blanket, she wore a small backpack made of cowhide that contained dried beef, some grain and dried fruit. Over each shoulder was a long strap attached to a lightweight hollow gourd. One gourd was filled with water, the other with honey-beer. As was the native custom, Mwalimu held a long walking stick in her left hand. It was made from the branch of an acacia tree and was about a foot taller than she was. On her right hip she wore a brightly beaded scabbard containing a short, broad sword about twelve inches long. She had provided the Salesman with his own blanket, backpack and drinking gourds.

As they walked and he began to comprehend the grand scale of the panorama in front of him, the Salesman also began to notice movement on the plains. He focused on these movements, and they resolved themselves into large herds of animals moving serenely through the grass.

The Salesman pointed. "What's that I see Mwalimu? I can see a herd of some kind over there but they're too far away for me to make out exactly what they are."

Mwalimu looked in the direction he pointed, shielding her eyes with her hand. "You're seeing a large herd of zebras mixed among a herd of wildebeests. It's very common for zebras to be at that spot this time of year. That's where we're headed—to get a better look at those zebras. Did you know that no two zebras are striped exactly alike? And for some reason, nobody knows why, zebras living closer to the equator are more boldly striped than others. Here we are very close to the equator so you will be seeing some of the best stripes that zebras have to offer!"

"That reminds me of something that happened just before I started this trip," remarked the Salesman. "I bought a new suit, a pinstriped suit. It's sort of the unofficial uniform for people in my business. Anyway, the salesman showed me a suit and said, 'These are some of the best stripes we have to offer.' Funny coincidence, huh? By the way, I bought the suit."   "Yes, a funny coincidence." Mwalimu nodded as they walked.

"They're beautiful to look at, but why do they have those stripes anyway?" he asked.

"You wear pinstripes to project a certain image for your business. Zebras don't wear pinstripes. The stripes that they wear might look beautiful, but they have little to do with image. They are a survival tool."

"A survival tool? To me, those stripes make them stand out. Wouldn't they want to be camouflaged so predators couldn't see them so easily?" he asked.

"An interesting question, Mwanfunzi. To you those stripes may look conspicuous. But it doesn't matter what they look like to you. Simba is the major predator of zebras. All that matters to the zebra is how their stripes look in Simba's eyes. During the day the stripes provide a protective optical illusion. They blend with the heat waves rising off of the plains and make the zebra appear to shimmer, making it difficult for the predator to see it, and the riot of stripes in a closely packed zebra herd makes it virtually impossible to distinguish an individual zebra. During the night, when Simba is more active, the zebras can move under the protection of the trees at the edge of streams and watering holes, then their stripes provide a camouflage pattern like the shadow of tree branches in the moonlight.

"The zebra's stripes can also teach us something about human nature which is important to your business. What do you think it might be?" she asked.

"Well for one thing it gives a whole new meaning to the saying 'you can't tell a zebra by his stripes,'" the Salesman said with a smile.

Then he remembered a mistake he had made not too long ago: About six months ago, a man called him to set up an appointment to discuss his investment situation. The caller wouldn't say how he got the Salesman's name so the Salesman assumed he had been referred by one of his other clients. At the appointed date and time, the Salesman's assistant walked into his office with an odd look on her face. She said that a man had walked in saying he had an appointment. The Salesman told her he was expecting the man and asked his assistant if there was a problem.

She looked a little uncomfortable and said, "He's not the kind of person you normally meet with. He looks like a bum. Besides he smells funny."

"Well that's just great," he sighed. "Send him in, will you. I want to get this over with quickly."

A moment later, in walked a man of indeterminate age. His gray, greasy hair hung out the bottom of a dark blue knit ski hat and poked through in tufts where the ski hat had holes torn in the material. He had a week's worth of whiskers on his dirty face. He was dressed in polyester plaid pants, well-worn running shoes without laces and a stained trench coat that was tightly buttoned all the way up to his chin, even though it was easily 80° outside. The man smelled like sour milk.

What have I gotten myself into? thought the Salesman. *This is going to be a giant waste of time. I gotta get this guy out of here quickly.*

The man took a seat in one of the guest chairs in front of the Salesman's desk. "Name's Albert," he mumbled.

Although the Salesman always made sure to shake hands with everyone he met for the first time, he didn't make any attempt this time. Who knew where Albert's hands had been.

"How can I help you Albert?"

"I got some money to invest. Whadya think I'm doing here?" the man said gruffly. His sarcasm was evident.

"Well, Albert, we do have certain minimum account sizes here..."

"I got plenty o' money."

"I'm sure you do, but investing is a complicated process. It's something you need to commit to for a long period of time. You can't just invest your money today and then change your mind tomorrow," the Salesman said and then thought to himself *because you need to buy a quart of cheap wine.* He spoke again, "You have to be able to leave the money invested for many years. And you can't invest all of it. You need to have a cash reserve and spending money."

"I got all the spendin' money I need. This money I wanna invest, I don't need it for nothin' else."

"That may be, but look Albert, I'm not sure I can be of help to you."

"Sounds like you don't want my business, Mister." He stood up and walked out of the office.

You got that right, Albert. **I don't** *want your business,* he thought as he breathed a sigh of relief. Then he called out to his assistant, "Got any Lysol to spray around in here?"

Three days later, the Salesman overheard one of the newer brokers in the office bragging about landing a $3 million account. The money was from an inheritance, and the heir was a character that looked like a vagrant and smelled like sour milk.

"There is a business lesson here," said the Salesman as he broke his gaze toward the zebras and faced Mwalimu. "Just like the zebra's stripes can confuse the lion about what he's actually seeing, people's appearances can deceive one another. I made a mistake when I misjudged a potential client, and it cost me a big account. Businesspeople need to be careful that they don't make the same mistake. When they evaluate a potential new client they can't be confused by the client's stripes.

"I need to find out clearly and completely what a person's needs are. I can't assume that I know what they want; they need to tell me. Until I know a person's needs I have no basis for determining *if* or *how* I can help him."

"Can you give me an example?"

"How about this. If I own a bookstore, I need to know what my customer wants to accomplish by coming to my store. Let's say the customer wants to change the oil in his car and needs to buy a

Business Jungle Survival Skill:

A four-step strategy to find out *how* to help a prospect.

Step 1: Ask questions that encourage the prospect to talk.
Step 2: Find out *if* you can help the prospect.
Step 3: Find out *how* you can help the prospect.
Step 4: Stop being a salesperson, start being a problem-solver. (You'll learn a lot more about this skill in chapters twelve and thirteen.)

new oil filter, then I know that I can't help him at all. But if he says he wants to buy a book about auto repair, then I know I can help him."

"Ah, yes," said Mwalimu. "But you don't know *how* you can help him, do you?"

"That's the reason I need to know all of his needs," continued the Salesman. "To find out, I need to ask him questions so he will tell me exactly what he wants to accomplish."

"What kind of questions would you ask?" Mwalimu was just testing him now.

"Questions that would encourage him to give me information. I'd ask him what kind of repairs he wanted learn about and why. I'd ask him what kind of car he wanted to repair, whether he was a beginner or an advanced mechanic. I'd ask him if he wanted a how-to book, a reference book or a textbook. After I had all the information, I would take him to the correct shelf where he would find the exact book to meet his need."

"That sounds like a very good selling strategy. Is it a strategy that will help you when you return to your office?"

"Yes it is. Whenever I understand a person's needs, I stop being a salesperson. I become a problem-solver and thus, a resource to my clients. When my clients view me in that role, I'm much more likely to earn their business now and in the future. That's a good business lesson."

"Excellent! That's your first lesson from the animals. Before this safari is over I think you will have more lessons about the importance of meeting clients' needs. Look, we're getting quite close to the herd. Let's see what else we can learn. Hush!" said Mwalimu as she lowered her voice to a whisper.

They crept slowly toward the edge of the zebra herd. "Won't they get nervous because we're so close?" whispered the Salesman.

"They will ignore us as long as they see our profiles. If we turn to face them they will gallop away."

Mwalimu signaled for the Salesman to sit on the ground. "Let's observe them from here.

"Zebras are the greatest advertisers in Tanganda," said Mwalimu. "The zebras that are holding their heads high are males. Their prancing communicates their virility to the females. The zebras with their heads and tails outstretched flat are females. That's the way they signal their availability to the males. These are just a couple of the many rituals the zebras use to communicate messages to the members of the herd. Naturalists call these rituals advertising. Zebras advertise more than almost any other species, and it is one of the reasons they have thrived while other species have become endangered."

"Advertising has a slightly different meaning in the Business Jungle," scoffed the Salesman.

"Does it really?" asked Mwalimu sharply.

"Of course it does! In the Business Jungle advertising means slick, glossy ads in magazines and newspapers and expensive ads on television—not prancing around trying to impress the opposite sex."

"The tactics may be different, but the strategy is the same. Isn't the purpose of

Business Jungle Survival Skill:

A four-step strategy to increase the herd with advertising

Step 1:   Determine your budget.

Step 2:   Determine the types of media to which your most important audience pays attention.

Step 3:   Create an important message.

Step 4:   Track results closely.

advertising to communicate a clear message to your most important audience about what you have to offer?"

She turned her attention back to the herd. "There are only three things that are important to the zebras: finding enough to eat and drink, getting away from Simba, and reproducing so that the herd will grow. Reproduction is the only one of those activities that must be done with another member of the herd. The only thing a male has to offer is his virility. The only thing a female has to offer is her availability. If the female is going to be successful at reproducing, she must send a clear message to her most important audience—the males—about what she has to offer. The males must do the same thing. If they don't advertise effectively then they won't reproduce and the herd will shrink. The zebras understand this, and their species is one of the strongest.

"The same principle applies to the Business Jungle. If you don't communicate a clear message about what you have to offer your clients then your business won't grow. How will potential clients know what you have to offer if you don't tell them?"

"But I do tell them. I'm quite good at turning prospects into clients. When they come to my office I have a pretty good presentation about why they ought to do business with my firm and me. About 50% of the people who hear my presentation turn into clients, and that's a great conversion ratio for my industry," boasted the Salesman.

"I don't mean to pop your balloon, but you missed the point," scolded Mwalimu. "The individual zebra is advertising to the entire herd, not to just one or two other zebras standing right in front of him. He wants to gather as many potential mates around him as possible. Think of advertising as the way you get those prospects into your office in the first place. Then once they are in front of you, your sales skills take over and you can convert them from prospects into clients. If you're really able to convert 50% of the people who you pitch to, why don't you want to increase the raw number of people hearing your presentation? Do the math, Mwanfunzi. Fifty percent of a larger raw number adds up to a lot more clients."

"I don't know if that'll work for me though. I'm just one person, and I don't get any advertising budget. Advertising is for bigger businesses."

"Irrelevant. Every business, regardless of size, has the same need: to tell its most important audience what it has to offer. If it doesn't, then the herd will get smaller. Period."

"Okay Mwalimu. I think I get it. It probably wouldn't hurt me to do a little advertising when I get home. It's expensive but probably not as costly as the business I never get because people don't know what I have to offer. If it works for the zebras, maybe it will work for me."

"There you go, another important lesson from the zebra. Now, let's move on, we have a lot more to see and do."

The Laws of the Business Jungle

3. Don't be confused by the stripes.
Learn to look through the optical illusions that make you unsure of what you are seeing when you evaluate a client or prospect. Find out clearly what the client's needs are, then you will know if and how you can help the client meet them.

4. Increase the herd with advertising.
The zebra must advertise to survive. You must advertise or your business could become endangered. Communicate a clear message about what you have to offer to your most important audience.

Chapter Three

WILDEBEEST TERRITORY

"Where to now?" asked the Salesman.

"We'll continue to make our way around the edge of the zebra herd until we find the wildebeests you saw earlier. Zebras and wildebeests often travel together, and gazelles often join them. Where you find one species, you usually find the others."

"Why is that?"

"Yesterday we talked about my partnership with the resort where you're staying. That lesson reminded you of the importance of alliances. The zebras, wildebeest and gazelles have an alliance, too. You might call it an animal alliance," Mwalimu explained.

The Salesman was intrigued. "An animal alliance, huh? How does it work? What's the benefit?"

"As they graze their way across the plains, the zebras feed on the taller plants and grasses. This method of grazing exposes the medium-length leafy grass favored by the wildebeests. When the wildebeests eat the leafy grass, they leave behind the short, fine grass which is the favorite food of the gazelles."

"That's a very clever alliance," marveled the Salesman.

"Yes, it is," said Mwalimu. "But it's more than just clever. Remember that everything these animals do helps ensure their very survival."

The Salesman was subdued. Then he said, "When you put it that way, my problem seems petty. I'm just not increasing my business as much as I want to, but these animals face problems that are much more basic."

"That doesn't mean that your problems are petty," Mwalimu asserted. "They are important to you and that is what gives them their significance. Don't belittle or minimize your problems. Honor them. In my culture we have learned to put these problems in their proper perspective. We believe that inside each problem is an opportunity waiting to be discovered. If you adopt this attitude, a *problem* metamorphoses into a *challenge*—a challenge to uncover the opportunity that is hidden within."

"That's a great philosophy!" exclaimed the Salesman. "I want to make sure I've got it right: 'Inside each problem is an opportunity waiting to be discovered. The challenge is to uncover the opportunity that lies within.' Is that it?"

"Yes. You have the first part right, but there's another important piece to it that I haven't told you yet. If you make a habit of viewing a problem through the filter of this philosophy, you won't avoid facing your problems. You will rush to embrace them because you recognize them for their inherent challenges. You will want to attack these challenges like Simba attacks a zebra, so that you can feast on the opportunity that awaits you."

"I can see how adopting this kind of attitude would make a huge difference in the way I do things. There have been times when I've tried to ignore problems in the hopes that they would go away. They never did. Usually they just festered and got worse. I'm making a promise to myself to try to adopt this attitude when I get home."

"Let me warn you that it won't be easy, Mwanfunzi. It seems that human nature is to dwell on the negative feelings that bubble to the surface of our minds when we encounter a problem. Adopting this attitude will take practice. When you encounter a problem the first thing to do is take a deep breath and avoid an immediate reaction. Then quickly think about what the hidden opportunity might be, then attack the challenge. Keep in mind, too, that you might not always be able to identify the hidden opportunity right away. That's okay, just keep thinking about it, and it will reveal itself."

"What the heck is going on over there?" asked the Salesman excitedly. He was pointing to a couple of wildebeests that looked like they had gone mad. They were bucking up and down, leaping and whirling in the air. They would dig their horns into the ground and toss up great clouds of dirt and dust. Then they would charge at one another shaking their heads and slashing with their horns but never getting close enough to inflict any damage.

"That bigger wildebeest is a dominant male, and that smaller, younger bull is attempting to move in on his territory," Mwalimu explained.

"But how can you tell where the boundaries of his territory are? The ground all looks the same around here, there's nothing to define the territory."

"You and I can't possibly discern the boundaries, but to the owners and the would-be usurpers the territory is very specific and well defined. The owners have drawn the boundaries, and they are as well defined as houses on fenced lots in a suburban subdivision. To protect their territories, the owners must continuously be on guard to fend off intrusions. After failed invasions, usurpers are banished to the outer edges of the herd. The dominant males will even run off unwanted females and their calves. They only permit a chosen few to remain in their territories. By successfully controlling and defending their territory, the dominant males prosper and so does the entire herd.

"This is a very good example of what survival of the fittest really means. There's also a good business lesson here among the wildebeests. The lesson has to do with defining and defending territory. How do you think the wildebeest behavior might help you in the Business Jungle?" she asked.

"Well, let's see. Businesspeople in any highly competitive industry need to be mindful of competitors who try to move in on their territory or take away their customers."

Mwalimu nodded in agreement. "That's correct, but let me add a thought here. As a businessperson, you are both the dominant male as well as the challenger."

The Salesman wore a confused expression. "I don't get that. What do you mean?"

"In the Business Jungle, competition between similar businesses creates something like a food chain. There are a few giant companies that truly dominate a given market. For example Charles Schwab dominates discount investment brokerage, Microsoft dominates software, and Exxon dominates petroleum. The other businesses in their industries are like young wildebeests trying to steal some of the industry dominator's territory. Those industry dominators have to spend a lot of their time watching for incursions and attempted invasions."

"I understand, but what does that have to do with me?" he asked.

"I'm getting to that part. I said that competitive pressures in the Business Jungle create a food chain. There is always going to be someone in your business who is bigger than you, and there will always be someone smaller. While you are trying to grow your business by taking territory away from those who are bigger or more dominant, you must simultaneously be aware of those who are smaller than you who want to take some of your territory. Does that make sense?"

An expression of understanding lit up the Salesman's face. "Now I get it. What you're saying is that whenever I gain any business, one of my competitors loses business. While I'm trying to get business from my biggest competitor, I have to watch out for someone who is trying to take some of my clients."

"Yes." She nodded affirmatively. "However, there's more to the story."

"What do you mean?" he asked looking confused again.

"Think about what you just learned about wildebeest behavior. First, they must set very specific boundaries that define exactly where their territories are. That way they know exactly what it is they are supposed to protect and defend. They cannot defend their territory unless they first define it," Mwalimu explained.

"Of course! First I need to define who or what my customer is. In other words, I need to figure out my market niche. That's *my* territory. When I know precisely what my territory is, then I can take steps to defend it." Mwalimu could almost see the light bulb shining above the Salesman's head.

"Absolutely!" Mwalimu patted the Salesman on the arm. "After you define your territory you'll be more successful at defending it. Do you know exactly what your territory is right now?"

"Well, I guess I define it as anyone who has money to invest in an amount that exceeds my minimum account size."

"Oh my, that won't do at all! You will have to do much better than that."

The Salesman was stung by the rebuke. "Why?" he asked sharply.

"That would be like the wildebeest claiming all of Tanganda as his territory. It would be impossible to defend that much land. It would be pointless to have such a big territory anyway because he would only be able to benefit from a small portion of it. Why try to defend territory you can't use? That's an exercise in futility. Later in our safari you'll learn a lesson from another animal about dominating your territory. For now, remember that your goal is to define a territory that is the right size for domination, maximize the benefits of it, and be able to defend it."

The Salesman sensed the wisdom of her words, and it salved the sting of the rebuke. "I need to be more specific about the kind of business I'm trying to get, instead of trying to appeal to everyone. Is that it?" He was eager to redeem himself in the eyes of his unexpected mentor.

"Now you're on the right track again! Good for you, Mwanfunzi."

"I'm glad I'm on the right track, but I don't really know what to do next."

"I am familiar with one of your country's greatest military leaders, a former Chairman of the Joint Chiefs of Staff who would have a good chance of being elected president, that is if he wanted the job. He once told me that a key to military success is to have a great plan, use the best equipment to execute that plan, and to care about the people that you lead. These are simple ingredients to business success, too. The General's advice can help you figure out what to do next."

The Salesman thought about the first ingredient in the General's advice: Have a great plan. Generals have battle plans. Football coaches have game plans. Architects have blueprints. Businesspeople need to have business plans. He reviewed in his mind the things he had learned over the years about writing a business plan. In order to be effective, business plans need to be written down. Keeping it inside the brain is not acceptable. The simple act of writing it down forces a businessperson to organize her thoughts completely. Business plans also need to be SMART: specific, measurable, attainable, relevant and time-bound. Recalling the lesson he had just learned from the wildebeest, he now knew that one of the prominent strategic elements in the business plan must be to specifically define the territory. In other words, he needed to define his niche. After his territory had been defined, he could begin to think about the tactical steps he would need to defend it.

Specific means that you avoid generalities, are clear and describe the elements of the plan with precision. For example, "my objective is to do more business" is not specific. On the other hand, "my objective is to increase my business by 20% over last year" is very specific.

Measurable means tracking performance. Only specifics can be measured, generalities cannot. How

Business Jungle Survival Skill:

All business plans must be *S. M. A. R. T.*

S*pecific*: Be precise

M*easurable:* Track progress

A*ttainable:* Be realistic

R*elevant:* Target correct market

T*ime-bound:* Set deadlines

is it possible to measure an objective like "I want to do more business"? How much is "more"? However, it's simple to measure an objective like "I want to increase my business by 20%." Now it's possible to keep track of the numbers and post them for reference. All business plans must frame their elements in a way that will make them measurable.

Attainable means that your goals are realistic. A goal such as "I want to double my sales by next week" is unrealistic and therefore unattainable. Constantly striving to achieve goals and objectives that are unattainable is terribly demoralizing and counterproductive. This makes the process of goal setting an intricate one. Goals should be set high enough so that they represent a stretch to attain but not so high that they become impossible dreams.

Relevant means that when the business plan is written, it reflects the steps needed to secure your market niche and your other sales goals. In other words, the plan is relevant to the niche you defined. If you decide that your niche is selling left-handed hairbrushes then you don't want to write a business plan that will sell right-handed combs.

Time-bound means that you set deadlines for your plan. Although it is the last letter in the acronym, it is of primary importance. Every goal, every objective, every element of a business plan must have a date, and sometimes even a time, by which it must be accomplished. This creates a sense of urgency about the implementation of the plan and also provides a measuring stick to look at how quickly, or how slowly, the plan is being implemented.

The Salesman used to write a business plan every year. He suddenly realized that it had been several years since he wrote the last one. He decided that he would write a new business plan when he returned home from this vacation. It was obvious to him that a lot of the ideas he would incorporate into the new business plan would be inspired by the experiences he was having on these abundant plains.

"Well, Mwalimu, my to-do list is growing longer and longer. I have a number of things to do when I get back to the office. When I write my new business plan it's definitely going to have a Tangandan flavor! You know, I'm almost looking forward to getting home so I can start work on all this new stuff."

"Yesterday you said you needed to get away from your business. Today you're saying you are looking forward to getting back. It sounds like you're changing your mind about whether I could teach you anything."

"I'm definitely re-thinking that opinion."

"That's very good to hear, Mwanfunzi."

The Laws of the Business Jungle

5. Inside each problem is an opportunity waiting to be discovered.
The challenge is to uncover the opportunity that is hidden within. If you adopt this attitude, you will embrace your problems because of their inherent challenge. When you discover the hidden opportunity you will feast on it.

6. Have a great plan.
Have a written business plan that defines your territory, then make an action plan that will defend your territory from competitors and maximize the benefits you receive from your territory.

Chapter Four

DANCES WITH DEATH

The Salesman and Mwalimu finished a leisurely lunch in the shade of the acacia tree. The temperature was steadily rising, but it rarely gets uncomfortably hot in Tanganda. Mwalimu suggested that they resume their safari to make sure they reached the Masara River before sunset. They wrapped up the remains of their lunch and placed them into their backpacks. After a final drink from their water gourds, they ventured out from under the acacia. Mwalimu led them along a well-trodden trail traveled by thousands of animals before them.

Mwalimu spoke, "We've observed two-thirds of the animal alliance I mentioned. Now we'll see the third partner—the gazelle. Gazelles are members of the antelope family, like the wildebeests. We'll see many different species today, but I especially want you to see and learn from the Thomson Gazelle. It has a unique survival skill.

"All of the many species of antelope have magnificent horns that are used for many purposes, from uprooting plants to dueling with rivals. But beautiful horns have also made antelopes a target for hunters in search of trophies," she continued. "One species, the Blue Buck, was hunted to extinction during the last century. Hunting pressure continues to threaten several species, but Africa still has more antelopes than any other continent.

"Since it is their fate to be the main food source for cheetahs, Tommies have developed unusual survival techniques. Adult Tommies are known for a behavior called 'stotting' which is quick, high, bounding leaps. They do this as a prelude to a full gallop, which reaches speeds of 50 mph."

"Fifty miles an hour!? I'm impressed." His expression made the Salesman's enthusiasm seem even greater.

"The obvious problem is that cheetahs exceed 70 mph. If the Tommies relied on speed alone, they'd never escape from a hungry cheetah in search of chow for dinner."

"So what do they do?"

"Rather than tell you, I'm hoping to show you," she replied.

The Salesman and Mwalimu continued along the trail. They reached several forks in their path but Mwalimu never hesitated about which trail to take. The sun continued its own safari across the spilt-milk sky and their shadows began to lengthen. Mwalimu slowed her path and broke the silence.

"Cheetahs often hunt in the afternoon, unlike most other big cats. Since it's not too hot today we might be fortunate enough to observe the death dance of the cheetah and the Thomson gazelle."

She then stopped walking altogether and scanned the plains in front of them, nodding in satisfaction.

"It seems that fortune is smiling on us. Look there..."

About 200 yards ahead of them a solitary male cheetah sat atop the remains of an old termite mound which was still about two feet high. From this position his predator's eyes gave him a wide-angled view of a herd of Tommies grazing about 150 yards upwind from his vantage point. The cheetah's attention was diverted for a moment by the sound of an approaching Land Rover.

The cheetah, who was accustomed to seeing the Land Rovers crawling across the plains, lost interest in it and returned his gaze to the herd. Most of the animals in the area had gotten used to the vehicles filled with wide-eyed tourists. The animals' experience with the vehicles has taught them that they present no danger. It was an easy task for the guide to maneuver his Land Rover very close to the cheetah's perch on the termite mound. When the guide judged that he was close enough, he parked the car and switched off the engine.

The cheetah casually glanced over his shoulder again to appraise the Land Rover. Then he slowly rose from his sitting position on the termite mound, arched his back in a typical feline stretch, yawned and nonchalantly sauntered toward the car. When he was close enough to the front fender, he lightly leapt onto the hood of the vehicle four feet above the ground, sat down and resumed his assessment of the Tommie herd.

The Salesman's eyes flew open in surprise, as did those of everyone inside the Land Rover. One of the guests stood up in the large open sunroof to snap a picture of the cheetah.

Turning to Mwalimu, the Salesman asked, "Why did the cheetah do that?"

Mwalimu just shrugged and said, "It's a better view from up there."

From his higher vantage point, the cheetah seemed to focus on a Tommie fawn that strayed farther from her mother than was safe. Never taking his eyes from the fawn, the cheetah jumped down from the Land Rover's hood and began slowly making his way closer. The target had been selected, the cheetah was committed and a young gazelle's life hung in the balance. The experienced guide realized that a hunt had commenced and that this was the sign to leave the cheetah to hunt unimpeded by the Land Rover's presence. The guide started the car and slowly drove off in the opposite direction.

The cheetah had now covered about 50 yards when the mother abruptly stopped grazing and jerked her head upright. At the mother's movement, the cheetah flattened itself in the grass. She had spotted the cheetah's motion and simultaneously noticed that the distance separating her from her fawn was uncomfortably large. Putting herself between the cheetah and the fawn, she casually resumed her grazing.

After a minute or two the cheetah resumed his stealth-stalk. The wind shifted. Now the cheetah was upwind of the mother and fawn. The mother caught the cheetah's scent on the wind, and her head sprung up in alarm as she was reminded of the danger in the grass. She looked around nervously trying to locate the cheetah, but this time she couldn't find it.

The cheetah's spots served him well, and he remained invisible to the mother and her fawn. The mother became more agitated; an unseen predator is the worst kind of threat. She glanced at the fawn, who remained unaware of the danger. Then the mother began stotting in a circle around the fawn. The movement caught the fawn's attention. She raised her head and then as if a signal had passed between her and the mother, the fawn lay down flat in the tall oatgrass.

Now the cheetah sat up but couldn't locate its prospective prey. This time the fawn's natural camouflage effectively concealed her from the predator. The cheetah scanned the grass trying in vain to reacquire his target. The fawn remained motionless in the grass and went undetected. Deciding that its primary target was no longer viable, the cheetah redirected its gaze toward the mother.

When the fawn lay down, the mother had begun stotting away from the fawn's hiding place and resumed grazing, showing little regard for the stalking cheetah. The mother was now the primary target, and the cheetah began the slow, patient stealth-stalk again. It appeared that the mother Tommie had forgotten about the spotted menace creeping through the grass, and the cheetah was making good progress toward her: crouch, two steps, down; crouch, four steps, down; crouch, seven steps, down. He was so intent on stalking the mother that the cheetah passed within three feet of the fawn's hiding place.

The Salesman whispered urgently to Mwalimu, "That fawn is gonna be his lunch for sure!"

The cheetah's attention was never diverted from the mother as it moved right past the fawn.

"What happened!" he whispered again. "Why didn't he pounce on that fawn?"

"Remember the unusual survival trait I mentioned? Now I'll tell you what it is. Tommie fawns have *no scent*. So, even though the cheetah was close enough to easily catch her scent, he can't smell her. In addition, the pattern of the camouflage in the fawn's fur is so well designed that she is invisible in the grass as long as she doesn't move. If the fawn moves however, then you're right, the fawn becomes lunch."

While they were talking, the mother periodically interrupted her grazing, moved farther away from her fawn and resumed eating in another spot. The cheetah continued stalking, and the mother continued her grazing-and-moving pattern until the cheetah was considerably past the fawn's hiding place. She settled down to munch a particularly succulent patch of grass and the cheetah crept quietly closer. When he was almost within striking distance, but before he could begin his

Business Jungle Survival Skill:

A three-step strategy for remaining focused and persistent

Step 1: Ask yourself every hour of the workday, *"What is the most important use of my time right now?"*

Step 2: Maintain your clarity of purpose. Ask yourself every morning, *"What is my highest priority today?"*

Step 3: Be patient. Business strategies don't always produce fast results. Persist with a strategy for a reasonable time before abandoning it.

dash, the mother bolted away in a direction perpendicular to her grazing path. In two giant bounds she attained her top speed of 50 mph. She was a quarter mile away in seconds, and the cheetah knew he had missed his target for good. He simply sat down and watched the mother run away, then he gazed around briefly blinking his eyes with a distinctly perplexed look on his face. A moment later, he sauntered off in a direction that took him further and further away from both the fawn and her mother.

Seeing that the danger was past, the mother returned directly to the fawn's hiding place. At the mother's approach the fawn stood up to greet her. Then mother and offspring continued their relaxed, but watchful, grazing. Their dances with death were over for now.

The salesman turned to Mwalimu with excitement in his eyes. "All right! Score one for the gazelles; they outsmarted the cheetah! What I just observed has profound applications in the Business Jungle. I want to clarify them in my own mind and tell you about them."

"That's wonderful, Mwanfunzi. Tell me when you're ready."

Mwalimu and the Salesman recommenced their trek along the familiar game trail they had been following before they had the remarkable encounter with the cheetah. The Salesman mentally massaged the vivid images of the stalking cheetah and the gazelle's triumph. The first lesson that formed in his mind was this: The cheetah was opportunistic. Even though it was not successful on this hunt, the cheetah took advantage of every opportunity that would increase his chances of success. At first the cheetah sat atop the ruins of the termite mound to get a better view of the gazelle herd. Then, when the Land Rover drove up, the cheetah realized that the view from the hood would be even better. An opportunity and an advantage had been recognized and the cheetah quickly seized it. By doing so, the cheetah placed himself in a position to be more successful.

The Salesman realized he (and every other businessperson) also needed to be opportunistic. He needed to be watchful for opportunities, recognize those that could give him an advantage, and then quickly act on them before they disappeared. But how would he recognize the most advantageous opportunities? How could he differentiate them from those that were disadvantageous? He thought about the cheetah again. The cheetah had a singleness of purpose: stalk and hunt down the Tommie. The only opportunity the cheetah seized was one that would propel him toward his goal.

Here was the answer.

The Salesman needed to have clarity of purpose. By keeping his purpose clearly in mind, he could seize only those opportunities that moved him closer to its achievement. Any opportunity that did not could be rejected.

The second lesson that came to his mind was from the gazelle. This lesson had to do with focus and persistence. The young Tommie fawn was required to focus intensely on its survival strategy of remaining motionless in the grass. If the fawn lost its focus for a second and made even a small movement, the cheetah's sharp eyes would have detected that movement and the fawn would have perished. Today the fawn was persistent and she survived. She will continue to survive as long as she remains persistent. These were valuable lessons for the Salesman. He thought about how indispensable it was to be focused at work. If unproductive issues distracted him, his efficiency would suffer and he would be less productive. He admitted to himself that lately he had lost his focus and persistence. His business development strategies had become erratic, and things going on around him in the office easily distracted him. This was a chief reason that his production levels had reached a plateau. He resolved to remain focused by frequently asking himself, *Is this the most important use of my time right now?* If the activity in which he was engaged was moving him closer to his objective then he could answer with a confident yes and he would know that he had the proper focus. The gazelle's lesson had reminded him that he must regain his focus and become more persistent if he was ever to climb off the plateau.

The Salesman shared these insights with Mwalimu. Then she spoke, "As a business-person you must always be running at top speed in order to outrun your competition, to catch up with prospective new clients, and to merely maintain ground with your existing clients. In the Business Jungle, you are both cheetah and gazelle, predator and prey. You must sym-bolically become a predator to hunt for new business from prospective clients and to stalk for cross-selling opportunities among your existing clients. You'll need the cheetah's speed to keep up with rapid changes in your clients' and prospects' expectations. You must anticipate these changes in expectations, not react to them. If you react to expectations, you will always be two strides behind your clients and prospects, plus you won't have the endurance to sprint long enough to close the distance between the two of you. When you anticipate changes in expectations, you must already have the product or service on the shelf to meet those new expectations. If you don't do these things then you, like the cheetah we saw today, will go hungry."

The Salesman listened to this enigmatic woman with amazement and with puzzlement, too. He was stunned by her translation of the parable's simple message into an indispensable principle of business success.

"Businesspeople are both predator and prey," Mwalimu continued. "If you are not the fastest one at sunrise, then you become prey for your competitors. You cannot stand still, you must make things happen. If you do not, then your competitors will run by you to claim your prospects and clients. You yourself will be nothing more than a limp body with a competitors jaws clamped firmly on your throat."

The mental picture Mwalimu painted for the Salesman gave him a brief chill, but it was powerfully pertinent—a sharp illustration of the importance of speedy proactivity as a survival skill in the Business Jungle.

Observing the cheetah and gazelles as they danced with death had proven to be a fascinating interlude, rich with meaning. The Salesman had witnessed the essence of the struggle for survival and distilled from it three new lessons that would serve him well when he returned to his work.

The sun was quickly moving toward the western horizon. It would be dark soon, so Mwalimu and Mwanfunzi hastened on their way toward their appointment with the Masara River.

The Laws of the Business Jungle

7. Be opportunistic

Be watchful for opportunities, recognize those that can give you an advantage, and seize them quickly if they will propel you toward your objective.

8. Focus and Persistence

Remain focused on your highest and best goals. Persist in the execution of your proven business development strategies and habits.

9. When the sun rises you had better be running—*fast*

Chapter Five

WARTHOGS ON WALL STREET

Mwalimu paused at the side of a shallow stream as they crossed the trail that was their path.

"This stream," she said, "has its origin in the hills to the south of us."

It ran cool and clear for about 15 kilometers before it wound its way to the Masara River. Both sides of the stream were covered with bushes and tall trees forming one of the dense riparian corridors that crisscrossed the plains. It was broad and shallow at the place where the stream flowed over the trail; the clear water was only three or four inches deep over the stony streambed. Both upstream and downstream of this spot the banks grew higher and closer together. The narrower streambed channeled the water until it quickly became three or four feet deep, and the small stones became large rocks and boulders. Because it was shallower at this point, it was a popular place for the animals to drink and ford the stream.

Mwalimu and the Salesman remained in the shade of the stream's trees as she studied the many animal tracks in the mud. She named the animals as she recognized their tracks: impala, waterbuck, bat-eared fox, hyena, Marabou stork and ostrich.

"A couple of warthogs crossed here very recently. They're moving in the same direction we are. I don't think they're too far ahead, and they don't move very quickly. We should be able to catch up to them. Ready to go?"

"If we must," said the Salesman lazily. "This really is a lovely spot. I could easily spend the rest of the afternoon here."

"All safaris begin with the first footprint in the dust of the trail. But it is not until all of the other footprints have been impressed upon the trail that the safari will be completed," Mwalimu counseled him.

"I get your drift. Let's go," he sighed. He was about to ask how she expected them to cross the stream without getting their feet soaked, but Mwalimu simply strode ahead until she was up to her ankles in water.

She must have been reading his mind again. "Those fancy shoes won't do you much good if they get wet. If I were you, I'd take them off and cross barefoot."

"I guess you're right; wait up a minute," he grumbled. He had paid nearly $200 for these hiking boots, which he had bought just for this trip from a yuppie outdoor clothing company. They really looked impressive, but they weren't even waterproof. He would've been better off buying a pair of $3 sandals made back in Mwalimu's *vijiji*. He regretted that higher price tags don't always mean greater functionality.

After he crossed the stream, he sat down on a rock to put his shoes back on. "Wait a moment, Mwanfunzi. I have something for you. I suspected you might need these before our safari was over. Now it seems like a good time to give them to you." She rummaged in her cowhide backpack and withdrew a pair of sandals.

"These may not have a corporate logo or the latest designer colors, but they will serve you well for the rest of your safari."

The sandals were simply and sturdily constructed from various sizes of leather patches that came from the hides of cattle raised by Mwalimu's people. The soles were made of many layers of the same thick leather; even the tough two-inch needles of the acacia tree couldn't penetrate through them. On top of the sole where the foot would rest, there was a single thin layer of ostrich leather that was luxuriously soft to the touch. Across the front was a half-inch strip of material under which the toes would slip and a smaller loop for the big toe. Farther back, an inch-wide strap was meant to go over the top of the foot just in front of the ankle. Attached to this inch-wide strap was a narrower strap, which went around the heel.

The whole system was adjustable using a small piece of bone that slid through holes punched in the heel of the shoe. They were exactly like Mwalimu's.

The Salesman slipped on the sandals and pulled the straps. They fit perfectly.

"I was just thinking about sandals like these. Let me guess, did your neighbor make them? How did she know my size?"

"Yes, my neighbor did make them. She's been making sandals for the people in my *vijiji* for 40 years. I knew your size because your driver asked your room attendant at the Safari Club to look closely at your shoe size. I spoke with the driver for a moment before we left this morning. He told me your shoe size. While we were gathering and packing our supplies, the sandal maker finished assembling your sandals. With 40 years of experience, she can finish a pair of sandals very quickly. My people can wear the same pair of sandals every day for many years. For you they will last much longer. Consider them my gift to you."

They did indeed last a long time. The Salesman dumped the heavy, hot, cumbersome, expensive shoes into his backpack where they remained until he got back to the USA. He wore the cool, lightweight, lithe sandals for the rest of his safari. He even wore them on the airplane during his return flight home. He felt a certain sense of pride about the sandals. They were much more than footwear. They were a connection to this land, these animals and to Mwalimu. When he wore the sandals, he felt closer to the Masara Masai region of Tanganda, almost as if he were a native himself, although he knew he could never really be one. Wearing the sandals was also his way of saying: I value the culture that would produce sandals such as these. I am proud to wear them. Thank you for sharing your values and traditions with me.

In the years after he completed the safari, the Salesman came to regard the sandals as symbols of all that he had experienced while he walked on the plains of the Masara Masai. He grew very fond of them. Whenever he was faced with a perplexing business challenge, he would put on his sandals and pace in search of the native wisdom that would help him overcome the challenge. The sandals seldom failed him.

"Thank you, Mwalimu. They are a wonderful gift," he said to her. The Salesman was really touched by her thoughtfulness.

Two pairs of feet in matching sandals continued along the game trail. In a quarter mile, the Salesman noticed that the ground to the right of the trail was churned up as if it had just been tilled.

"The warthogs have been busy," Mwalimu commented. Then she pointed, "Look, there they are."

Standing in the middle of the trail about 25 yards away, staring straight at them, were two warthogs. There was an air of cockiness about the two of them as they stood blocking the trail. The salesman thought that it seemed as if they were taunting him. If they could have spoken, he was sure they would have had a Brooklyn accent and said: "What are you lookin' at bud? You lookin' at *me?* You wanna come down this trail, you're gonna have to go through me an' my pal here. You wanna piece of us?"

The warthogs were the ugliest critters the Salesman had ever seen, inside or outside of Tanganda. Mostly they looked like large pigs, except their legs were longer. They had very long coarse hair that grew in a ridge down the middle of their backs and fell four of five inches down their sides. There were occasional clumps of this bristly hair on various parts of their bodies, most notably at the end of their short tails. The most striking feature was their huge, grotesque heads. Those heads! They were exquisite. They were dazzling. They were overwhelming in their ugliness!

Their heads were so large as to be completely out of proportion to the rest of their bodies. The Salesman laughed out loud as a mental picture formed in his mind of a warthog that could no longer bear the great weight of its monstrous head. In his mental picture the warthog's head hung down with its nose on the ground. It's front legs were buckled so that it rested on its knees, and its body was so unbalanced that it tilted far enough forward so that its rear legs were lifted completely off the ground. Those little airborne hind legs were running like mad and getting nowhere, while its hairy tail spun around furiously like the rotor of a helicopter.

Of course, Mother Nature had recognized her design flaw in the warthogs and had given them massive necks and shoulders to compensate for the huge head. Not only did the disproportionate size of their heads contribute to their ugliness but so did the assorted lumps, bumps and other bony contusions that disfigured their faces. These protuberances were described as warts by the first explorers to see them and thereby became the poor animal's namesake. Two of these warts, located on either side of the mouth near the upper jaw, sprouted enormous, wicked-looking tusks. The total effect of the large, warty head combined with the sharp tusks and aura of cockiness was one of formidability and intimidation.

"By your smile, I see that you've been smitten by our lovely warthogs," Mwalimu said with a grin.

"Well, I wouldn't rush to take one home to Mother," the Salesman replied.

"What do you suppose they use those fearsome tusks for?" she asked him.

"You're asking me? Ohhh, wait a minute, this must be the start of another lesson."

"Could be, Mwanfunzi. So, what are those tusks for?" she persisted.

"I don't know for sure," he began slowly. "But I'd say they were for digging. They couldn't be four-legged rototillers. I'll bet they use them for fighting, too."

"Those are excellent guesses. In fact those are important uses for their tusks. However they are secondary to a much, much more important use."

"What might that be?"

"Image and attitude."

Mwalimu went on to explain that a warthog without tusks would simply be a big, hairy pig and that no self-respecting warthog would ever want to be mistaken for a hairy pig.

"The tusks are a status symbol. For males, the tusks declare their virility. A male with substandard tusks would be shunned by females and picked on by the other big-tusked males. A great set of tusks means that the females will flock to him while his potential rivals give him a wide berth. Conveying a sense of image and attitude is the most important function of a warthog's tusks."

The Salesman nodded his head in agreement. "For that purpose the tusks work very well. When I first looked at this pair I was definitely struck by their image and attitude."

Mwalimu continued, "If you think about what you've observed you will appreciate the lesson the warthogs have offered."

The Salesman considered the warthogs and then with a shrug he said, "I just don't see what warthogs have to do with my job in the investment world of Wall Street."

"I thought you would have figured out this lesson right away. Let me help. How important are image and attitude to the success of a businessperson?"

"Naturally they are very important..." he began, but stopped in mid-sentence. Then his jaw dropped and his eyebrows shot up as enlightenment showed in his face. "Ah-hah! Now I get it!"

Consumers have certain expectations about how their grocer, salesman, physician or barber should look and act. These expectations exist for every person or organization they might do business with. Consumers make a decision to do business based on how well they think a businessperson will meet their expectations going forward. A very big part of that decision-making process is based upon how they perceive the businessperson's image and attitude (I&A). If the I&A sends the right message, then the consumers' comfort level rises and they will make an affirmative buying decision.

When a consumer has been converted to a customer, retaining the customer's business is determined by how well the businessperson actually meets the expectations. Of course, when the customer first meets the businessperson, he has no idea how well she will actually perform, but the decision-making process has to begin somewhere. The customer is willing to give her a chance if he approves of her I&A.

Here's the bottom line: *Obtaining* business depends on I&A. *Retaining* business means meeting the customer's expectations in the delivery and performance of the product or service.

Unfortunately, this decision-making model is a superficial one. Superficial or not, the Salesman recognized this as a basic law of the Business Jungle. Potential new customers will form their initial impressions of him within the first few seconds of meeting him. During those first few seconds, I&A speaks much louder than his credentials and education, training and experience or even the price he charges for his product or service. He must understand and obey this law of the Business Jungle if he wanted to survive there.

This was the realization that dawned on the Salesman. It was not a new realization; he had known these things for a long time. But the lessons of the warthog gave him a new appreciation of the seriousness of I&A. Now he shifted his thinking somewhat and began to consider the ways in which image and attitude personally affected him.

He recalled a recent personal decision he had made not to do business with a physician. It happened several months ago after he had injured his knee while jogging. The soreness and stiffness lingered for a long time. Finally, after six weeks of discomfort, he asked his family physician for a referral to a knee specialist. He remembered that his decision not to hire the physician was based upon her failure to meet his I&A expectations during their first, and only, appointment. The Salesman's expectations fell into two categories: the I&A of the medical office, its staff and its office procedures and the I&A of the physician herself.

His expectations were fully met regarding the office and staff. The office was modern, tidy, well equipped and comfortable. The staff was friendly, courteous and efficient. However, his expectations regarding office procedures were not met. His specific expectation was that the physician see him promptly at the appointed time. He would tolerate small delays and would even forgive tardiness due to extreme emergencies. He refused to be kept waiting for 30 or 40 minutes or more simply due to poor scheduling. One reason he still had the same family physician for more than ten years was because his doctor always saw him within 15 minutes of his scheduled time. On those rare occasions when he was delayed, the physician never failed to acknowledge the delay and apologize for the inconvenience.

On his first visit to the knee specialist, it was twenty-two minutes after his scheduled appointment time that he was ushered into a small consultation room, and it was six minutes longer before the physician walked in to introduce herself. Although she was unaware of it, she was close to losing this new patient before she could send the bill for the first visit. The Salesman still had not made his buying decision one way or the other. The extent to which his expectations would be met in the next few moments regarding the I&A of the physician herself would finalize his buying decision. These were his expectations:

1. A knee specialist should appear to be physically fit, and all doctors should appear to be in good health.
2. She would probably be wearing a white lab coat, but it would be fine if she weren't.
3. Since he was meeting her for the first time, she should introduce herself in a polite manner by saying her first and last name with a firm handshake. (It would be the kiss of death if she insisted on referring to herself as Dr. So-and-So. Real people have first and last names.)
4. She should talk to him in terms he could understand, not medical jargon.

When the doctor walked in to the consultation room 28 minutes had elapsed and she had one strike against her, but the Salesman was willing to let her stay at the plate to take a few more swings. The doctor was between 45 and 50 years old and was tall and slender, her tanned face and hands suggested she spent a lot of time outdoors. She wore high-quality running shoes, on her wrist was an unpretentious runner's watch and she appeared to be quite athletic. She was wearing a white lab coat with long sleeves, lapels and two buttons in the front. It was nicely tailored to look like a sport coat rather than a smock. Her name, Dr. S. Jones, M.D., was embroidered in red above the breast pocket. She wore a dark blue polo shirt underneath with the shirt collar spread over the coat's lapels. The Salesman made these observations in about three seconds. So far, so good.

"Hi," she said. "I'm Dr. Jones. It's nice to see you. Let me just take a look a moment to review your chart, okay? Hmm, looks like you've got retro-patellar pain syndrome going on here, emanating from the medial side of the right knee."

When she introduced herself she did not offer to shake hands, nor did she care to mention her first name. For all he knew, the "S" in the Dr. S. Jones, M.D. that was embroidered on her lab coat could have stood for Susan, Sally or Sarah. But he suspected that it stood for Stuck Up. She made no eye contact with the Salesman because she was flipping through the pages of his medical chart. There was no attempt to build rapport before

they got down to business, no apology for her lateness. When they did get down to business, she spoke to him in terms he had no hope of comprehending.

The Salesman thought *Uh-oh, this physician is showing signs of terminal expectation failure.* This brief exchange had taken about 25 seconds. During that time the doctor failed to meet the Salesman's expectations regarding the manner in which she introduced herself (Strike two!), and she failed to

Business Jungle Survival Skill:

A four-step strategy to assess your I&A:

1. Identify expectations held by customers and prospects.
2. Assess how well the expectations are being met.
3. Implement needed changes.
4. Reassess, now and forever.

meet his expectations regarding the way she communicated with him (Strike three! Y'er out!). Once he had actually met Dr. S. Jones, it took less than 30 seconds for the Salesman to finalize his buying decision. The rest of his appointment took about 20 minutes, but it made no difference. It would've made no difference if Dr. S. Jones graduated first in her class from the best medical school, or she did more knee repairs than anyone else in the universe, or even if she had written the most authoritative text about his exact medical problem. The fact was that Dr. S. Jones had struck out, and the Salesman would not be coming back to see her again. All because of I&A.

When the Salesman told his story to Mwalimu she agreed that his experience with the physician was a good real-life example of the warthogs' lesson about I&A. Then she asked him to think some more about the warthogs, but this time to consider how the lessons applied to his personal business.

"What kind of I&A do your customers and prospects have of you, and how well do you measure up?" she asked. She fixed him with a penetrating stare and admonished him, "When you consider this, you must be brutally honest with yourself, otherwise don't waste your brainpower."

The warthogs had lost interest and had moved off the trail into the grass. The Salesman and Mwalimu resumed their walk with the Salesman lost in thought. As he began to self-assess his own I&A, he instantly realized that it would be a worthwhile exercise for any businessperson.

Step 1: Identify expectations

Every prospect and existing customer has expectations pertaining to I&A; they just have different expectations for different types of businesses. The businessperson's first step in self-assessment is to identify the particular set of expectations that prospects and customers have for his particular business. *Okay, sounds simple,* he thought, *but how do I do it?*

As he pondered this question, he stopped to watch an iridescent green beetle as large as his thumb crawling purposely along the path. He carefully stepped over the beetle and then decided that there were at least three sources of information about what peoples' expectations of him might be.

First was intuition. The Salesman was certain that he and every other businessperson already has (or should have) a pretty good idea of what customers I&A expectations might be. He had to turn this idea into a written list.

Second, he needed to ask existing customers what their I&A expectations were when they first made their buying decision. He had to turn that into a written list, too.

Third, he could get professional help. There are plenty of self-help books available on marketing, advertising, public relations and sales. He could do some research. There are also many highly qualified consultants available for hire to help gather and analyze information about peoples' expectations. Large companies often have in-house departments to perform this function. A combination of some or all of these sources will provide all the information a businessperson will need.

Step 2: Assess

The second step in the I&A self-assessment was to evaluate how well he lived up to the expectations identified in step one of the self-assessment. This is where Mwalimu's admonition about honesty applied; if he was not honest with himself about this evaluation then he'd be wasting his time because the results would be bogus. Assuming that it is done honestly, the evaluation itself is rather simple.

In his mind's eye he envisioned an evaluation matrix. Along the left-hand edge were listed each of the expectations identified in step one. Below were five columns labeled to correspond to a degree of success in meeting each expectation: "Did Not Meet," "Met Some, But Not All," "Fully Met," "Exceeded Some," "Exceeded All." Using the matrix was as simple as putting a checkmark in the appropriate column for each of the expectations. The completed matrix would quickly and easily pinpoint how well he was meeting the I&A expectations.

Business Jungle Survival Tool:

I&A Self-Assessment Evaluation Matrix

Expectation	Did Not Meet	Met Some	Fully Met	Exceeded Some	Exceeded All

Step 3: Implement

At this point, up popped another question: *Who's supposed to actually fill in this matrix?* The answer became evident quickly, the same three sources he thought of in the first step. He could fill it in himself, existing customers could do it or professional consultants could do it. The Salesman realized that in many cases when businesspeople rate themselves, they are too critical which results in undeservedly low scores. On the other hand, existing customers, especially *satisfied* customers, are often too generous in their assessments resulting in undeservedly high scores. Either outcome paints a false picture. That's why an impartial consultant acting as a "secret shopper" might provide the most realistic scores.

Once the data has been entered on the matrix it can be analyzed for strengths and weaknesses and an action plan can be created. This is step three of the four-step process.

While completing this step the Salesman thought that he should give himself a pat on the back for each check mark he put into the categories labeled "Fully Met," "Exceeded Some," or "Exceeded All." High ratings such as these mean that he's doing something right and that's worth being acknowledged and enjoyed.

After a little celebrating, the Salesman could then turn his attention to the really meaningful and exciting part of the matrix. Here lay the expectations that were not met or partially met, and here is where the most improvement and progress can be made. The analysis of the matrix should zero in on these lower scores. This portion of the I&A self-assessment reminded the Salesman of the philosophy of *hakuna matata*, which also meant that *inside every problem is an opportunity waiting to be uncovered.* Unmet I&A expectations are the problem. The opportunity is creating and implementing the action plan that will eventually raise the ratings to "Fully Met" or above.

The Salesman explained to Mwalimu the I&A self-assessment process that he envisioned. As he explained the first three steps Mwalimu listened with the same intensity she had shown earlier.

"Just think," he said when he had finished explaining step three, "if I complete step one correctly, I'll know what my customers' and prospects' expectations are *in advance.* In step two, I will have honestly evaluated how well I meet their expectations. Plus, I'll *already* have a plan in place to make sure I continue to meet those expectations because I carefully implemented step three. After I do all this I'll write my action plan that contains specific steps to raise each rating.

"My I&A rating is going to be off the scale; it's going to be pretty hard *not* to do business with me. Any businessperson has got to love that!"

"Don't get too carried away yet, Mwanfunzi. You didn't tell me about the fourth step yet, and it's significant."

Step 4: Reassess

The final step is the ongoing habit of performing regular, periodic implementation checkups. The Salesman recognized that the checkups could be used to make two determinations. First, how completely was the action plan implemented? In other words, did he do what he said he would do? Second, how effective were the specific procedures he implemented? In other words, did they work? Did they result in his ability to meet or exceed an expectation that was previously unmet?

If the first checkup determines that the action plan has not been fully implemented then it will serve as a wake-up call that the Salesman needs to refocus and quit procrastinating. If the plan has been fully implemented, then the second checkup will determine its effectiveness. Rising rankings as a result of the action plan mean that the whole process is a success. Yippee! Pat on the back!

However, if the desired outcome, higher ratings, is not achieved, then the action plan needs to be tweaked. A new and different set of procedures will need to be written into the action plan in order to achieve the desired outcome. The two checkups will need to be completed repeatedly until the entire action plan is implemented and all the procedures are achieving the desired outcome.

The Salesman verbalized these thoughts to Mwalimu and added a final caveat. "I learned earlier today from the cheetah and gazelle that survival is like a circle. I've also learned that this I&A self-assessment is not a linear process; it's also circular. In order to remain effective the process needs to start over again at step one as soon as step four is complete."

"Those are excellent insights, Mwanfunzi. You are exceeding *my* expectations about how much I thought you would learn on this safari. I guess I'll have to revise my expectations and set higher standards for you to achieve, raise the bar as they say." Once again she gave him an approving grin and a pat on the arm.

The Laws of the Business Jungle

10. The Importance of I&A

Prospective new customers have expectations about I&A. If you meet or exceed their expectations they're likely to do business with you. If you don't, they won't.

Chapter Six

THE WISDOM OF WILD ONIONS

Mwalimu and the Salesman continued their comfortable walking pace along the trail. Mwalimu wanted to revisit their discussion about I&A.

"I think my next question will be a tougher test of your insight."

"Fire away!" the Salesman exclaimed.

"You have learned well from the warthogs about the importance of image and attitude. You have made an important connection between the warthogs who live in the middle of nowhere, as you are so fond of saying, and your Business Jungle at home. You clearly understand the 'how' and the 'why' of I&A, but I wonder if you understand the 'when.' So, this is my question: When should you be most concerned about meeting the I&A expectations of a customer or prospect?"

"That's not such a hard question. I thought you were gonna really zing me!" he said with a small sigh of relief.

"I advise against being overconfident, Mwanfunzi. The answer to this question may surprise you," Mwalimu cautioned.

"You only get one chance to make a first impression. I think I should be most concerned about meeting the I&A expectations beginning within the first few seconds of my first meeting with a customer or prospect," he responded confidently.

"Please define *first meeting*," she asked quickly.

"That's when I have the first face-to-face appointment, either in my office or at the customer's office or home."

Mwalimu nodded her head, but her approving grin had vanished. "That's a good answer, but it most certainly is not the best one. If you don't worry about I&A expectations until you have your first appointment with the customer or prospect, you're too late. It doesn't matter when *you meet them* for the first time. What really counts is when *they meet you* for the first time."

"I don't get the distinction. When we have our first appointment we meet one another at exactly the same instant."

"Mwanfunzi! Suddenly your thinking on this is too superficial. I have raised the bar for you and I know that you have the ability to leap over this hurdle, but you'll have to take another run at it. Right now your thinking falls below the level of the bar."

As she spoke, Mwalimu stooped to pull a weed out of the ground at the side of the trail. The weed had 10 or 12 tall, slender, tube-like stalks each about 12 inches long. These stalks were dark green at the tips and faded to white where they entered the dirt. The Salesman thought the weed looked vaguely familiar. Mwalimu brought the weed over so he could look at it closely and he detected its pungent aroma. He recognized five onions the size of golf balls at the root of the weed.

"These are the wild onions that grow in some parts of Tanganda. Learning the truth of this lesson is like peeling one of these onions." Mwalimu twisted one of the onions off the stalks and peeled away the first layer. "So far you have peeled away only the top layer of this lesson. I want you to keep peeling the onion until you can answer my question about the 'when' of I&A. Talk to me again when you think you have the answer."

She held out the rest of the onion and dropped it into the Salesman's upturned palm. She put the four remaining onions into her pack, explaining that they would make a good addition to their evening meal. Then she turned her back on the Salesman and resumed walking up the trail.

The Salesman stared at the partially peeled onion in his hand. *Well,* he thought, *you certainly impressed the old gal with that clever answer!* Then he hurried along to catch up with his mentor and guide. He followed three or four steps behind Mwalimu as they continued along the trail. While he walked, he pondered and absently picked at the onion in his hand.

He puzzled over this lesson. There was something odd Mwalimu had said that could help him peel this onion. What was it she had said? Then he remembered: *It doesn't matter when **you meet them** for the first time. What really counts is when **they meet you** for the first time.* What did she mean by this? It was cryptic. Why was it not important when he met the prospect? How could he and the prospect do anything other than meet each other at the same time? It wouldn't be much of a meeting if there was only one person in the room! A prospect couldn't meet him without him meeting the prospect. But then he had this nagging thought: *or could they?*

The Salesman felt that he was on to something. The harder he thought, the more he picked at the onion. Figuratively speaking a prospect *could* meet him without ever being in his physical presence and shaking his hand. A layer of the onion peeled away and fell out of his hand to the ground, but he didn't notice.

He was sure he was on to something now. As he warmed to the subject, he decided there were lots of ways that prospects could meet him without him meeting the prospects. He labeled these *unilateral meetings* because they really do take place with only one person in the room (that person is the prospect). The next revelation was startling for the Salesman: *Unilateral meetings are even more consequential than face-to-face meetings.* He was confident about the import of this revelation because during a unilateral meeting the prospect may make decisions about him and his business without his being in attendance and without him being able to explain himself.

Now his thoughts were cascading like the water tumbling downstream over the rocks where they forded it.

Since he is not able to represent himself in a unilateral meeting, it is critical that the information in the possession of the prospect must meet or exceed the prospect's I&A

expectations. If it fails to meet these expectations, the prospect will almost certainly make an unfavorable buying decision and the Salesman wouldn't have an inkling that he was even in the running to possibly earn the prospect's business.

Another layer of onion fell away and landed in the dust.

The Salesman was becoming a little uncomfortable with this notion of unilateral meetings. He had no control and could exert no influence over these meetings. This was the source of his discomfort, he didn't like being out of control. Too bad his next thought made him even more uncomfortable. *Unilateral meetings can happen at virtually any time or any place, and he would have no clue when or where they were happening.*

Almost immediately, he thought of three ways these unilateral meetings could happen. Prospects could attend a unilateral meeting in which they would figuratively meet him without ever being in his physical presence by:

1. Looking at his business card
2. Reading a letter he wrote
3. Listening to his voice mail

He was certain he could uncover more ways to have them happen if he

Business Jungle Survival Skill:

The four-step I&A self-assessment process can be used to meet the prospect's expectations *in advance* during a unilateral meeting.

thought about it long enough. Right now, he only wanted to think through these three.

Any of his prospects could do any of these three things at any time and in any place. Each time it did happen, the prospect would have certain I&A expectations about how the business card looked, the professionalism of his letter or the manner in which the telephone was answered. The extent to which he met those expectations would determine whether he had earned the right to a bilateral (face-to-face) meeting with the prospect.

Several more layers of the wild onion fell onto the trail, but they went unnoticed by the Salesman and were crushed under one of his sandals.

As usual, Mwalimu was right. It really was more important when the prospects met him for the first time, because they could meet him weeks, months and even years before he ever physically met them. That's also why she said it would be too late if he simply started worrying about meeting I&A expectations at the first appointment. Since he couldn't control the time or place of these unilateral meetings, it was imperative that he properly manage the I&A expectations in advance.

An onion layer sloughed off.

Okay, he said to himself, *how do I manage these expectations in advance of even meeting the prospect?* The answer revealed itself immediately—the four-step I&A self-assessment. When he had conceived the four-step process he had only considered its application in terms of the first appointment. Now that he had discovered the concept of the unilateral meetings, he could see that the four-step process was equally applicable to managing expectations in advance.

Now the Salesman redirected his deliberations to the three ways prospects could have a unilateral meeting: a business card, a letter or a telephone call. It was possible to apply the four-step process to each of the potential meetings to help ensure that he was anticipating and meeting I&A expectations every time. Every businessperson can do the same thing. Different businesses have different ways in which unilateral meetings might potentially occur. For the four-step process to work effectively, each businessperson must carefully consider all the ways those unilateral meetings might occur and assess each of them.

This is good stuff I'm coming up with here, he mused. *I'm on my way to redeeming myself with Mwalimu. But before I tell her any of this I had better be sure I've thought it all the way through.*

Once again, he considered the three potential unilateral meetings. First on the list were his business cards. Every time a prospect read his business card a unilateral meeting was taking place and the prospect had I&A expectations that must be met or exceeded. The Salesman was surprised by the realization that he handed out thousands of business cards each year. Over the course of his career, he had put at least 50,000 business cards in circulation. Handing out a business card is a bit like putting a note in a bottle and throwing it into the sea; there was no way he could know how far that card would travel or into whose hands it might fall. Regardless of how they traveled, his business cards represented 50,000 potential unilateral meetings. He had better be darned sure they met I&A expectations!

He made a mental note to do a complete I&A assessment of his business cards when he got back to his office. But while he was walking, he did the assessment in his head. He remembered the four-step process:

Step 1: Identify expectations. What kind of expectations would his prospects have pertaining to his business cards?

Step 2: Assess. He honestly felt that he fully met these expectations.

Step 3: Implement changes. In this case, since he fully met expectations he didn't need to make any changes. Although he was happy that his business cards rated a "Fully Met" assessment, he wasn't satisfied with it. Later, he would take steps to move the assessment toward "Exceeded All."

Step 4: Reassess. He would faithfully reassess his business cards every year to make sure that they still met expectations.

In the process of handing out all those business cards he had received many in return. Most of those also deserved a "Fully Met" rating, too. A few were deserving of "Exceeded Some" or even "Exceeded All" ratings. Unfortunately, some were definitely in the "Did Not Meet" category. From this, the Salesman concluded that neither he nor any other business-person should *ever* take their business cards for granted; they simply generate far too many unilateral meetings. If the business cards provide poor I&A, then the businessperson is abruptly shot down in flames. All businesspeople need to regularly perform checkups on their business cards.

Next, he needed to assess expectations about his correspondence. Once again, the sheer number of letters he sent each year struck him. His habit was to send at least five letters per day to prospects. That alone was over 1,200 letters a year. This doesn't count all the letters in which he attempted to cross-sell his existing customers. Between these two types of letters, he had had several thousand unilateral meetings.

What then were the prospects' expectations regarding the letters he sent? How about these:

♦ They should arrive as first-class mail, not bulk rate or third class.

♦ They should be individually addressed, never addressed to "Dear Sir or Madam."

♦ They should never have typos; the content of the letter should be short and to the point.

The Salesman critiqued his correspondence relative to these expectations and reluctantly concluded that it rated as "Met Some." He judged that he met all of the expectations with the exception of the last one. Lately the content of his letters had lacked punch. It wasn't that his letters were overly

Business Jungle Survival Tool:

A four-step I&A self-assessment worksheet for evaluating your business cards

Step 1: In column 1 of the table on page 70, write the expectations your customers, clients and prospects have for your business cards.

Step 2: Place one checkmark in columns 2 - 6 indicating the degree to which the expectation is met. *Be honest!* Next, assign an overall rating of your assessment. If the overall rating is "Fully Met" or higher, move on to the next item you want to assess. If the overall rating is below "Fully Met," go on to steps 3 and 4.

Step 3: For each expectation that is less than "fully met" write down at least three action steps you will implement to raise your assessment. Then, write down the date by which you will implement the action steps.

Step 4: Each of the action steps you listed in step 3 must be reassessed to ensure that they are effec-tive. Write down a date that is three months after you implement each action step; this is your reassessment date. On this date repeat step 2.

long, but the all-important opening statements could be more vigorous. He didn't always describe the benefits that helped the customer understand his service or product and his call to action lacked a sense of urgency that would motivate the customer to act quickly. Since his correspondence was assigned a substandard rating it was placed high on his to-do list and he would thoroughly address this challenge, and the opportunity that it presented, soon after he got home.

Business Jungle Survival Tool:

Use this matrix for steps one and two.

Expectation	Did Not Meet	Met Some	Fully Met	Exceeded Some	Exceeded All

Overall rating: _____

The third way a unilateral meeting can take place is by telephone, or more specifically by voice mail. The Salesman spent the biggest part of his day talking on the telephone. In fact, it took up 50-60% of his time at work. Even though using the telephone was an intimate part of his day, he had not figured out a way to have more than one conversation at a time.

When he was engaged with a telephone conversation, he was therefore unavailable to anyone else who attempted to call. The mathematical reality was that an incoming caller had as much as a 60% chance of getting a busy signal. This is clearly an unacceptable situation.

In an attempt to address this challenge, the Salesman's firm had installed a fancy voice mail system with the ability to answer a virtually unlimited number of incoming calls. Like many businesses, the Salesman's firm thought that voice mail was the answer.

A scenario sprung into the Salesman's mind which prompted him to have a conversation with himself: *Let's say that one of my prospects has a unilateral meeting generated by one of my business cards or letters, and let's say that her I&A expectations are at least "Fully Met" and she decides to give me a call. Now we're getting somewhere! But what is going to happen as soon as she finishes dialing my number? Chances are 60/40 that she's going to talk to my voice mail before she ever talks to me.*

The Salesman stopped in mid-stride as this realization formed in his mind and he perceived its implications. Mwalimu glanced over her shoulder and saw that he was stopped in the middle of the game trail. His eyes were unfocused as he looked inward. She noticed that he dropped a piece of the onion as he stood there in mute surrender to the synapses staccato surges throughout his brain. A faint smile formed

---

Business Jungle Survival Tool:

Use this for steps three and four.

Expectation that needs improvement:

_____

Action step 1: _____

Action step 2: _____

Action step 3: _____

Target implementation date: _____

Target reassessment date: _____

on her lips as she moved into a small patch of shade cast by a banana tree. There, she waited patiently for her Mwanfunzi to finish his mental wrestling match.

Meanwhile, the Salesman was oblivious to Mwalimu and the game trail, even to the fact that he was in the middle of the Masara Masai on a safari. He had embarked on a mental safari sparked by the warthogs' lesson about I&A and he didn't like where it was taking him. He was beginning to comprehend the astounding implications of his new realizations about his voice mail, and he was also beginning to feel apprehensive because he feared that he had made some colossal blunders. Frankly, he had never really thought about his voice mail before —just as he had never pondered the nature of his coffee maker or his stereo. It was just *there*, like any other appliance. Now he was grasping the nature of voice mail and the potential impact that this appliance could have on his business. When a prospect finally went to the trouble to call him, the reality is that it was quite likely that she would reach his voice mail and yet *another* unilateral meeting would take place. The prospect would have yet *another* opportunity to form a buying decision based on how well he met her I&A expectations, expectations focused on his telephone manner.

The Salesman shuddered to think that he could meet or exceed the prospect's I&A expectations of his business cards and correspondence, only to fail at the end when the prospect finally called him. What a shame to be so close to actually talking to the prospect, yet still so far! Voice mail is not an appliance at all. It is a vastly important business development tool that has a far-reaching impact on his success. It can either move him closer to converting a prospect into a customer or forever destroy the possibility of the conversion. Too many businesspeople underestimate voice mail's ability to make or break business development strategies. Nor do they understand its ability to actually propel the business development process forward and so they underestimate its power.

Now that he firmly grasped the true nature of voice mail, the Salesman's mind raced ahead to assess his own voice mail proficiency. Once again, he had begun to slowly walk down the game trail but was still fathoms deep in thought. When he reached the shady spot where Mwalimu waited, he passed by her unawares. But barely three paces later, he again stopped, prevented from further movement by the resumption of the wrestling match in his mind.

So many of his mental faculties had been brought to bear on the lesson at hand that his brain was, for the moment, unable to process the instructions necessary to keep him walking ahead on the trail. His overloaded nervous system was shunting power to the places where it would help the Salesman process his thoughts. As he stood there, he began to list what I&A expectations for voice mail might be. They were surprisingly simple; he was certain that any prospect would expect: a personal greeting in the Salesman's own voice, context for why the call was not being answered personally, and a reward for taking the time to make the call in the first place.

How well did I meet these expectations? he asked himself. The honest answer was unsettling: "Did Not Meet" was too good a rating for his voice mail. A rating of "Just What Was He Thinking" would have applied nicely. The sad fact was that his voice mail was nothing more than telephonic junk mail. This was a problem that deserved the highest priority and needed immediate attention. As soon as he got back to his tent cabin at the Masara Safari Club he would dial-in to his voice mail and make some changes.

The first change would be to record a personal greeting. The Salesman never seemed to find the time to record a voice mail greeting in his own voice. It was such a bother to think of something clever to say and then figure out how to push all the right buttons so that the technology would work correctly. He had to admit that he was a bit intimidated and embarrassed by the whole process. As a result, it was much easier for him to use something called the system greeting, which was an impersonal, prerecorded message in an anonymous voice that reeked of indifference. He grimaced to think of all those prospective new customers calling him only to hear an unsympathetic, synthetic voice say, "The party you have called is unavailable. Please leave a message at the tone." Yikes! It was crystal clear that his voice mail greeting *always* needed to be in his voice.

The next change would be to provide information within the greeting that would set the context for why the telephone was not answered personally, suggest alternatives and provide additional information to help the caller set future expectations. He would set the context by saying why he couldn't answer the phone. For example, *I'm with a customer* or *I'm on a business trip.* He would help set future expectations by saying when he would return the call: *I'll be back next Monday* or *I'll call you back today before 5:00.* He would suggest alternatives for the caller: *Please leave a detailed message,* or *Press "0" to talk with my assistant,* or *Call again at your convenience.*

The third change to his voice mail would add a benefit statement to his greeting so that the caller would receive something of value in return for making the call. This benefit statement could be quite simple: *Evening and weekend appointments available so you don't have to interrupt your workday,* or *Now you can access your account on the Internet whenever it's convenient for you,* or *Complimentary customer seminar coming up in two weeks—ask for details.* When he was a rookie salesman his sales training manager had given him some good advice. She said, "Always be selling. Never miss an opportunity to tell someone about a benefit you can provide to them." The Salesman recognized that his voice mail could be a powerful selling tool, not merely an answering machine, if he always had a greeting that contained a benefit statement. He was sure that this would make his old sales training manager quite happy. If voice mail is misused or abused it can become a business killer. If it is used properly it can be a business builder, for any kind of business. With that final thought, the Salesman resumed his walk down the game trail. When he took his first step he felt a piece of the onion fall out of his hand and bounce off the top of his foot. He had forgotten about the little onion Mwalimu had given him. He opened his hand to look at it, but all he found was a tiny piece no bigger than an almond. He looked at his feet and saw an onion layer in the dirt next to his sandal. Then he turned and looked behind him along the trail; at irregular intervals he saw more layers of the onion littering the path.

I'll be, he thought. *I guess I've peeled away the layers of the "when" of I&A, just as Mwalimu had asked. Now I'm ready to answer her question.*

The Salesman cleared his throat and said, "Mwalimu, based on what's left of this onion, I think I'm ready to tell you the rest of my thoughts about I&A..."

When he had finished explaining about the "when" of I&A, Mwalimu's approving smile had returned to her face. "I knew you would clear the hurdle. You've peeled away all the layers of this lesson and have a thorough understanding of the importance of I&A," she announced happily.

"I guess that warthogs do have a place on Wall Street after all, right there alongside the bulls and the bears," the Salesman added.

"And don't forget the wild onions! Seriously now, if you will take my counsel I will tell you this: Remember the warthog and ask yourself, *am I projecting the right image and attitude or will I be mistaken for a big hairy pig?*"

The Laws of the Business Jungle

11. The "When" of I&A

Anticipating and meeting I&A expectations begins long before your first appointment with a prospect. Unilateral meetings can occur at any time or any place, and you must prepare for them in advance.

Chapter Seven

SONG OF THE HIPPO

Mwalimu and the Salesman walked side by side on the familiar game trail. Their shadows trailed behind them, stretched out long and skinny by the almost horizontal rays of the slowly sinking sun. It was that honey flavored time of day just past afternoon, but not quite dusk, when life began to slow down and things began turning to gold. Mwalimu estimated that they would reach the Masara River just as the sun kissed the horizon and bid the earth good night.

As they walked, Mwalimu quietly explained the secrets of the countryside. She spoke of the medicinal value of some plants and trees; the difference between harmless, benign insects and those that were armed with biting, stinging or venomous defenses; which types of soil could be turned into clay and shaped into useful vessels and which types would give up its pigment to decorate their masks or faces.

The Salesman studied Mwalimu's face as she spoke reverently about the land. It was a face blessed with tranquility. Her eyes reflected a quiet confidence born of accumulated experience that had aged into wisdom. A clear and untroubled expression said *I know who I am and I am at peace with myself.* The Salesman yearned for her to reveal the secrets of her life even as she revealed the secrets of the countryside. People at peace have no need to talk about themselves, and so none of her life's secrets were offered. He knew there was no point in asking again. Mwalimu was helping him write the chapters of a survival guide for the Business Jungle, but the cover to her autobiography remained firmly closed.

Meanwhile, the spilt-milk clouds reflected a solar sponsored symphony of celestial light. He saw a crescendo of color softly changing from white to yellow to gold to amber to orange and finally to pink. The time was drawing near for their appointment with the Masara River.

"Welcome to the Masara River, Mwanfunzi. This is the halfway point of your safari, and here we will spend the night. This is the same river you see from the Masara Safari Club. The resort is about 40 kilometers downriver."

The trail they had been following brought them to the edge of the river and in front of them gaped the gorge of the Masara. It was 150 yards across to the opposite bank and 50 feet down to the water's surface. The river itself was 60 yards wide; in the middle of the channel the water was 6 feet deep. It was rich with silt carried all the way from Tanzania giving it the color, texture and consistency of milk chocolate. The current could hardly be detected.

Although the river moved slowly at this point the Salesman decided that describing it as languid would be a mistake. "Languid" suggests that the river had an absence of energy, a laziness. Such was not the case. True, the river did not have all the froth, foam and frenzy of a white-water river; rather it flowed with the calm confidence borne by the eons that the river had spent etching its gorge on the face of Tanganda.

He decided that "placid" was a better way to describe the calm and peaceful river, yet he resisted using that label, too. Like a pair of shoes a half-size too small, "placid" was a close fit but it just wasn't right. He gazed at the river and it conveyed a sense of inevitability to him. The inexorable mission of the Masara River was to shape the earth, deepen the gorge and patiently carry away its burden of silt. For time out of mind the Masara had been unremitting in its pursuit of its single purpose, and it would remain so eternally.

This very timelessness rendered the label placid as inappropriate. Placid was far too tenuous a description; it belied the permanence of the river. Serene was the next word that came to his mind. Now *that* was a good word for this river—serene. The Masara's calmness and timelessness was far too great to be discomposed. The Salesman decided that he would label the Masara River as serene. It was an exact fit.

From upriver came a strange, almost mournful sound that interrupted the Salesman's labeling. He looked toward the source of the sound; he saw what looked like a fleet of ten or twelve partially submerged Volkswagen Beetles floating around a bend in the river. It took a moment for the Salesman to realize what he was seeing and interpret the odd sound. It was a herd of hippos coming down the river. He felt rather silly that his first impression of the hippos was that of a little German car. The fact is that the hippos are bigger than the cars and the cars are much cuter than the hippos. As they came down the river, they huffed a resounding "mwaa, mwaa" that was somewhere between a grunt and a moo. It was the hippos' grunt/moo that had distracted him, and he recognized it as the same sound he heard while he sat in the bar at the Masara Safari Club.

"Mwalimu," he said excitedly, pointing toward the herd, "look at those hippos! They're huge!"

Several of the animals separated from the herd and lumbered up onto the shore. They looked comically awkward as they plodded toward a tasty clump of grass.

"That is the least graceful animal I've ever seen," chuckled the Salesman.

"They do seem that way, don't they?" Mwalimu replied. "Walt Disney displayed an ironic sense of humor when he choose to depict hippos as ballerinas in *Fantasia*. Don't you agree?"

"Oh yeah, I love that movie. That part with the hippo-ballerinas is hilarious. But I didn't think Disney movies would get much screen time out here. How did you see *Fantasia*?"

"It doesn't matter how I saw it..."

"...only that you did see it." He finished her sentence for her.

"Thank you, Mwanfunzi, that's correct. Now, about the hippos. You may be surprised to learn that this amphibian is actually one of the most dangerous creatures in

Tanganda. Hippos are the second deadliest animals in Taganda. They kill many people each year. My people respect all of the animals that live here in the Masara Masai. Some of them we both respect and fear; the hippo is one, and there is one other."

"You gotta be kidding! One hardly thinks of hippos as fierce killers."

Mwalimu explained that the hippo's awkwardness on land turns to grace and speed in the water. A fully grown hippo weighs more than two tons, but when it's in its aqueous element, the river buoys its great bulk and the hippo can run along the riverbed at great speed. The buoyant beast's mouth is two feet wide, and its jaws are strong enough to bite a canoe (or a man) in half with a single chomp.

Bulls are ferociously aggressive when guarding their territory and their harems. While many animals guard their territories with ritualistic displays of aggression, the hippos' aggressiveness frequently escalates into bloody battles. Often these fights are to the death.

Females are equally aggressive when protecting their calves.

The nature of the hippo is the antithesis of the nature of the river. As much as the river is serene and composed, the hippo is savage and uncontrolled. Its great size, speed, agility in the water and fierce disposition make it a formidable force of nature in Tanganda. They dominate the Masara River. One study estimated that every 100 yards of riverbank was home to 20 hippos.

Business Jungle Survival Tool:

A four-step strategy for defining your territory

Step 1: Write down the definition, as you perceive it right now, of your market niche / target market / territory.

_____

_____

The remaining steps of this Survival Tool will follow later in the chapter. (Don't jump ahead.)

They dominate the river so completely that the native people fear to use the river themselves. There is no fishing here, no canoeing, no gathering of water or laundering of clothes. There is only the hippo, content with its brutal dominance of the Masara.

The Salesman was dumbfounded by Mwalimu's description of the hippos. He was awestruck by their mighty dominance of their territory. In the midst of his wonder he began to recognize the emergence of another law of the Business Jungle. His mind flashed back to their morning encounter with the wildebeests. While he studied the wildebeests, Mwalimu had told him about the General's keys to success, one of which was *have a great plan.* While watching the wildebeests, the Salesman had given a lot of thought to the ingredients of an effective business plan. Then, he had concluded that his business plan must define his territory by defining his market niche. Now, through his observation of the hippos and Mwalimu's surprising description of their behavior, he refined and expanded the role of the business plan. The overriding goal of a business plan must be *dominance.* He (and every businessperson) should strive to do nothing less than dominate their market niche, just as the hippos dominated the Masara River. When he dominates his market, his competitors will hesitate to dip their toes into the water of his river.

"An excellent observation, Mwanfunzi. It was my hope that the hippos of the Masara might provide this lesson about dominance," she replied after he gave a voice to his thoughts. "A question, please."

"By all means, but I hope it's not as tricky as your 'simple' question about the 'when' of I&A!"

"Tell me, Mwanfunzi, how would a business plan help you achieve dominance? What is the business plan's single most important task?"

"That's two questions. But it doesn't matter; they're excellent ones. This time I'm going to think carefully before I reply, give me a moment."

"Take as much time as you need. We'll walk no further today; we'll camp on this spot. Looking out over the river at sunset is soothing to the soul and relaxing to the mind.

Relax. Listen to the river and the hippos—they can tell you much. Now give me your backpack, blanket and gourds so I can begin to set up our camp."

The Salesman handed his things to Mwalimu and she busied herself with campsite chores while she happily hummed the tune of a native chant. The Salesman walked to the edge of the gorge and sat with his feet dangling over the precipice. The sunset symphony had blazed through an octave of rising colors and was building toward an orange-pink finale. The river at the bottom of the gorge had fallen deep into shadow but the remaining light from the falling sun was enough to allow him to see the hippos basking, floating, reveling in the river that was theirs. His mind drifted.

What was the business plan's most important task...listen to the river and the hippos...

The sun dropped below—over the edge of the earth in a final timpani drum roll of radiance and the Salesman had a sunrise of understanding. While they were watching the wildebeests, Mwalimu had said that he would learn from another animal about dominating his territory. That animal was the hippo. She had also said that you can't defend a territory unless you first define it.

Once again the huffing/mooing/grunting of the hippos interrupted his contemplation. He glanced over his shoulder and saw that Mwalimu had gathered a handful of leafy stalks from some kind of bush. A mosquito buzzed by his ear, he turned to swat it and faced the river again.

Listen to the hippos and the river...

The hippos have defined their territory as the Masara River. Each bull has further defined his territory as a specific strip of shore and water. It is the very specificity of the definition that allows for the dramatic degree of dominance that the hippos enjoy. For the Salesman and other businesspeople, *territory* means the same thing as *market niche, market area, target market* or any of the other terms used to identify the group of clients to which products or services are sold. If there is no definition of the territory, there can be no dominance—simple law of the real jungle, simple law of the Business Jungle.

The Salesman was now certain that the most important task of a business plan was to define the territory. The river and the hippos had told him so.

He continued watching and listening to the masters of the Masara River. The pop and crackle of a newly built campfire sounded behind him. Reluctantly, he left his listening post at the edge of the gorge and joined Mwalimu beside the fire.

"Were you able to hear the song of the hippo and the whisper of the river?" she asked.

"Yes I was, and now I have answers to both of your questions."

"Wonderful. You can tell me while we eat. But first, help me prepare our dinner."

From within her pack she produced a small ceramic pot. She instructed the Salesman to fill it halfway with water from a water gourd and then to set the pot on the coals until the water boiled. When it was ready he would add two handfuls of the grain they had brought and remove the pot from the coals. While they waited for the water to boil, Mwalimu unsheathed her short sword and deftly sliced the onions she had found, using a fallen tree as her cutting board. She also diced some of the leafy stalks she had gathered explaining that they had a flavor similar to basil.

Heat from the hardy campfire brought the water to a roiling boil. The Salesman added the grain and set the pot on the ground outside the fire ring. For the next 15 minutes the grain absorbed the water as it softened and expanded. Then Mwalimu added the onions, pseudo-basil and dried beef to the pot. Finally she added some honey-beer and replaced the pot on the coals to simmer all the ingredients together.

While their dinner simmered, they each selected a spot to unroll their blankets. The Salesman was getting ready to unfurl his blanket when Mwalimu stopped him.

"A word of caution —if you sleep there you'll be sharing your bed with fire ants. That small mound by your right heel is their home. When they are disturbed they instantly swarm to the attack by repeatedly biting anything they perceive to be an attacker. Their venom is most unpleasant."

"I appreciate the warning."

"Just trying to help. I put my blanket between the fallen tree and the fire ring because of the direction of the prevailing breeze. Where you are standing is downwind of the fire, so you'll be breathing smoke all night. Over here I'm upwind of the fire, and with the tree behind me it will make an effective windscreen if the breeze picks up. Why don't you come over here, there's plenty of room for two blankets."

The Salesman stepped carefully around the anthill and relocated his blanket in the space between the tree and the fire ring.

"Dinner should be ready shortly. If you want to wash up, there is a small stream about 50 feet down that path. It would be a good place to do laundry if you're so inclined."

"I think these clothes will last another day without washing. I didn't bring any hand soap, have you got any?"

"The kind of soap you're used to would be bad for the stream. Use this instead." Mwalimu handed him the thick root of a native plant.

"Break open the root and use the liquid inside like liquid hand soap. It will clean your hands quite well, soften your skin, and it won't hurt the water quality of the stream."

Ten minutes later, the Salesman walked back into camp feeling fresh after washing his hands and face in the clear, cool stream. As Mwalimu had promised, the soap root worked as well as any factory-made product.

"Perfect timing. Come, dinner is ready," Mwalimu said brightly. "Let me serve you what I call Tangandan Stew."

Meat, grain, honey-beer and spices had bubbled and blended to make a rich and flavorful stew. Mwalimu and the Salesman sat on the fallen tree and enjoyed the meal. As they ate, the Salesman told Mwalimu about the lessons that the river had whispered and that the hippos had sung to him.

"So, I think that there is a single answer to your two questions. A business plan can help any businessperson dominate a territory by thoroughly defining the market niche, and it is the creation of the specific definition that is also the business plan's most important task."

Mwalimu nodded as she ate, and the Salesman continued.

"What I need to remember is that the success of my business plan depends to a great extent on the strength of the definition—it must be precise."

He paused to savor a mouthful of Tangandan Stew.

"This morning, when we observed the wildebeests, you were critical of me because I defined my territory as anyone with money to invest. I now see that this is a weak definition because it lacks specificity. It's impossible for me to be all things to all people. That would be like one hippo trying to claim the entire Masara River or one wildebeest trying to claim the entire savannah as its territory. If I try to get new business from anyone with money to invest, I'll spread myself too thin, lose my focus and be ineffective. But if I'm specific about my market niche I can focus like a laser

Business Jungle Survival Tool:

A four-step strategy for defining your territory, continued from page 82

Step 2: Re-think the definition you wrote in step 1. This time make it highly specific, and write it down.

Step 3: Now repeat step 2, aiming for even greater specificity. Keep repeating step 2 until you can't refine your definition any further.

Step 4: When you're satisfied with your new definition, post it where you will see it every day.

beam. This law of the Business Jungle applies to every kind of business I can think of, not just mine. Unfortunately I've been doing the opposite—and so have a lot of other businesspeople."

"What are you going to do about it, Mwanfunzi?"

"Well, I've already decided that I need to write a new business plan when I get home. The first thing I'll do is spend time refining the definition of my territory. When I'm satisfied with my definition the rest of the business plan will follow. My goal is to become the hippo in my territory; I want to dominate my stretch of the river."

The Salesman swallowed and held his breath. He searched Mwalimu's face for a reaction to what he had just said. He remembered his disappointment when Mwalimu had called his thinking in regard to image and attitude "superficial." It was not a mistake he wanted to repeat. Not only did he want to avoid being disappointed with himself, but he also realized to his surprise that he didn't want to disappoint Mwalimu.

Finally Mwalimu smiled at him and said, "You listened well to the river and the hippos. I think that perhaps you *will* become a hippo in your own part of the river. For that to happen, you'll have to remember more than the song of the hippo and the whisper of the river. You'll need to remember all the lessons that the animals have shown you and you'll need to obey the laws of the Business Jungle which embody them."

The Salesman breathed a sigh of relief; this time his thinking measured up to Mwalimu's high level of expectations. He was glad that he hadn't let himself or Mwalimu down.

"You know, I think I learned more today than I have on any other single day of my business life. Yesterday, when I met you, I really didn't think you would teach me anything. I was conceited enough to think I knew all there was to know about business. I felt so superior that I thought that a native woman like you couldn't possibly know enough to teach me anything. Even if by some fluke you were a good business coach, I saw no way I could learn anything from you out here, in the middle of nowhere. I was wrong. I'm sorry."

Mwalimu moved over to sit next to him on the fallen tree. She patted his knee. "No need to apologize. A little skepticism is a good thing. It helps prevent us from doing something foolish."

They sat in silence for a while, watching the campfire's flames dance and the coals pulse with heat. As the darkness of the African night descended, a chorus of insect hymns rose to greet it.

Tomorrow you'll learn many more things as we complete the safari and return to my *vijiji*. I suggest we get some sleep so we can get an early start. Besides you never know what might happen during the night that could awaken us."

"That sounds ominous! What do you mean?"

"It's nothing, don't worry about it. Do you want to brush your teeth? I promised to show you how to do it in the native fashion."

"Sure. I always brush before bedtime. No exceptions, even when I'm on safari."

"Then let me show you how to make a safari-style toothbrush."

Mwalimu selected a half-dozen stems she had picked earlier from some kind of plant. The four-inch stems had a number of leaves on one end. She bound the stems tightly together around a small stick to make a small bouquet with a cluster of leaves at the top. She handed it to the Salesman.

"This is called "myrrh." Native people have used it for ages to help clean their teeth. You use it just like a toothbrush. The leaves are the 'brush' part, and the 'toothpaste' is built into the leaves."

The Salesman inspected the toothbrush closely, grimaced, and stuck the wad of leaves into his mouth as if it were his regular toothbrush. When he had finished brushing he had a surprised look on his face.

"That was terrific!" he said "Simple and effective. Maybe I'll throw away my toothbrush when I get home and tell my dentist that he should start growing myrrh in his waiting room."

The darkness of the night was complete on the plains that surrounded them. The light pollution caused by man-made illumination didn't bleach away the night sky on the savannah. As the Salesman settled into his blanket bedroll, he lifted his eyes to the velvet canopy above. The stars were like diamonds scattered across the vast black velvet sky by some cosmic jeweler. He tried to recognize the unfamiliar constellations that inhabited the sky south of the equator. Very soon his eyes became heavy. He was physically tired from the day's walking and he was mentally tired from processing all of the lessons he had learned. When he dropped off to sleep, he was thinking about the laws of the Business Jungle.

The Laws of the Business Jungle

12. Define your territory.

The most important task of a business plan is to define your territory—your market niche. The strength of the business plan depends on the strength of the definition. The strength of the definition depends on its specificity.

13. Dominate your market.

The goal of your business plan is to seek dominance of your stretch of the river. If you dominate your market, then your competitors will hesitate to put their toes in the water.

14. Brush your teeth with myrrh.

Chapter Eight

THE LION'S SHARE

The flames of the campfire had dissolved into a bed of glowing coals. The embers throbbed with red heat as the final fragments of wooden fuel were consumed. Lying on his side facing the campfire, the Salesman slept soundly and dreamt.

He was a dream-bird flying above the grassy plains of the Masara Masai. Perhaps he was a brilliant starling, an ibis or maybe even an African condor. His wings held him effortlessly aloft as he used the thermal air currents as his highway.

Thrilled by the intoxicating freedom of flight, he descended swiftly and skimmed over the top of the grass. He dropped over the edge of the Masara River gorge and plunged to the water's surface. Flying three inches above the water, he swerved left and right as he threaded his way through a herd of hippos and approached the far wall of the gorge. He shot upwards at a 90° angle to climb up the face of the wall and rocketed over the top of the gorge like a trick pilot in a flying circus.

When he leveled off, he found himself 100 feet above a herd of zebras. They appeared nervous. Their ears were cocked forward and they anxiously stared at a trio of lionesses standing nearby. The lionesses started walking toward the zebras. Their walk morphed into a trot and then broke into a full run. The zebras wheeled in terror and bolted away from the charging predators, toward a nearby riparian corridor lushly overgrown with bushes and trees.

An instant later, the bushes exploded into shards of leaves, twigs and dust as three more lionesses launched themselves toward the zebras. Ambush! Once again the zebras scattered in terror and confusion as they sought to escape the deadly claws and fangs of the big cats. The lionesses accelerated into the midst of the confused herd; the thrill of the hunt shone in their eyes.

They roared as they ran, an ear-splitting, earth-shattering roar that rose above the plain to where the dream-bird hovered, watching in grisly fascination. He felt the awful power of the roar reverberate all the way to his bones. The power of it was palpable; it made him dizzy, disoriented. His wings went limp and he began to spiral down to the ground, sinking deep into the terrible bellow...

The Salesman's eyes snapped open. In a heartbeat, he was fully awake and leapt out of his bedroll. He heard the roar again, only this time it was no dream. With his heart racing and adrenalin flooding his veins, he shouted to Mwalimu.

"What is that? What's happening!?"

Mwalimu was at his side in a second. She placed a protective arm around his waist.

"That is Simba, Mwanfunzi. Do not worry; we are quite safe. The roar is Simba's way of celebrating a successful hunt tonight. The sound of the roar has traveled several kilometers to reach your ears and disturb your sleep."

"But it sounded so loud, so close!"

"Simba is a powerful animal. His roar can be heard for many kilometers on a clear, calm night like tonight."

"Are you sure we're safe here?"

"I am certain of it. We are in no danger. Simba will be busy for a day or two consuming the kill. It may be a week before he hunts again. Besides, I told you that Simba fears my people. I have no fear of lions, but I respect them and I know how they behave. We are safe."

"I believe you, but I'll feel a lot better when it's light."

Mwalimu glanced at the star-strewn night sky. "It's still at least four hours until sunrise. You should get some more sleep."

"Yeah, well, I think I had the sleep scared out of me just now. I'm going to stoke the fire and sit up for a while."

"Suit yourself, Mwanfunzi. I'm going back to sleep. Don't be surprised if you hear more roars tonight. In the morning I'll tell you more about lions and how they can teach you to survive in the Business Jungle."

I'm just worried about surviving the night! he thought as he stirred the coals of the fire and Mwalimu crawled back into her bedroll.

Hours later, Mwalimu gently shook the Salesman to wakefulness. He noticed that the sun was just above the horizon. The campfire had been rekindled and water was just coming to a boil in the small ceramic pot.

"Well, well Mwanfunzi" she smiled at him. "We survived the rest of the night without being swallowed by Simba. How did you sleep after our nocturnal serenade?"

"Once I finally fell asleep I guess I slept okay," he replied as he sat up and rubbed his eyes.

"Good. Would you like coffee? We grow a lot of coffee here in Tanganda; it's quite good."

"Expensive, too. At least in the USA."

"Yes, I know. Most of what we grow is exported to Europe and the USA. Not many of the local people drink it, but I like a good cup of coffee in the morning. Started drinking it many years ago. I brought a small package of coffee along; it was roasted just the day before yesterday. Care to join me?"

"I'd love too; I like coffee in the morning, too."

Mwalimu handed him a wooden bowl of the hot, rich, aromatic Tangandan coffee. "Would you like to hear more about Simba, Mwanfunzi?"

"Sure. I might as well know more about the critter that gave me such a rude awakening."

Mwalimu took a sip from her bowl of coffee and began to explain leonine behavior.

Most lions of the African grasslands live in groups called "prides." A pride is a complex society that consists of up to 30 members. It includes adult males, a number of females and assorted offspring. The lionesses within a pride are often related, with sisters, cousins, daughters and mothers living and hunting together. The male's role in the pride is simple: protect the pride from other males, mate with the females, sleep a lot, hunt a little, and consume a disproportionate share of the food. This disproportionate sharing is where the term "the lion's share" comes from. The female has other roles: bearing the young, caring for and raising the cubs, performing 80-90% of the hunting, submitting to the will of the males, and so on.

The Salesman snickered and said, "That arrangement sounds like the division of labor in many human families; the women do all the work."

"I've often thought the same thing. Now if I may continue. When lionesses hunt they do it very differently than the cheetah. The lionesses hunt as a team, while the cheetah is a solitary hunter. Although the styles are distinctive, one style is not necessarily more successful than the other. Cheetahs and lions must work hard for their meals. Only about one in four hunts ends in a kill.

"A common hunting technique used by lions is called 'stalkers and killers.' Several lionesses will conceal themselves in tall grass or bushes downwind of a herd of zebras, or other prey. These are the 'killers.' Other lionesses, the 'stalkers,' will circle around behind and upwind of the herd and then drive the herd toward their concealed sisters who are waiting in ambush."

Here the Salesman interrupted Mwalimu's explanation. "Let me guess what happens next. When an unlucky zebra is within striking distance the killers will explode from their hiding places to bring down the zebra."

"Why, yes, that's correct. How did you know that?"

"I had an interesting dream last night. I'll tell you about it some time."

Mwalimu gave him a curious look and resumed her narrative.

"Using their great strength and weight, the lionesses will bring down the zebra and strangle it by clamping strong jaws on the throat and collapsing the windpipe.

"Now recall the cheetah's style of hunting. A lone cheetah sitting atop its vantage point selects a target. Then with great patience and persistence the cheetah will slowly creep toward the target until it's close enough to make the final, furious 70 mph strike.

"So you see Mwanfunzi," Mwalimu concluded, "the hunting styles are different. Each style is suited to the needs of the respective species. The lion relies on teamwork. Different team members have different roles and each must perform their role properly or the hunt will fail. The cheetah relies only on itself, all of its hunting instincts, such as target selection, patient and persistent stalking, and a final burst of speed, must mesh perfectly or it will have an empty stomach. A lion can't hunt like a cheetah, and a cheetah can't hunt like a lion. People, however, are not limited to a single hunting style. In the Business Jungle you can, and should, use both styles of hunting for new business."

The Salesman shrugged his shoulders, "Yeah, well, I'm not in the habit of crushing people's windpipes."

"Of course not. All of the lessons you are learning about the laws of the jungle have symbolic application to the Business Jungle. Even though you won't apply these laws literally, they can still help you get the lion's share of the business in your territory. Businesspeople who know and obey the laws of the Business Jungle will have a higher survival rate than those who don't."

"I've certainly learned some important survival skills to help me earn more clients. When I stepped on to the airplane in Detroit I was really at a loss about what to do to jump-start my business. I certainly didn't expect to find any answers out here, but I'm getting a good education. I also know that you wouldn't have given me such a lengthy explanation of the big cats' hunting styles without there being some kind of new lesson involved. Am I right?"

"Yes, you are right Mwanfunzi." Mwalimu's eyes always brightened when a lesson began. "A lesson about business development lies among the sharp fangs and claws of the cheetah and lion."

"Don't tell me! Let me figure out what the lesson is. It seems to me that when a lion and a cheetah are hunting that it's analogous to when a salesperson prospects for new business. Depending on the situation the salesperson might prospect lion-style, or he might prospect cheetah-style. That's what you meant when you said both styles of hunting should be used. How am I doing so far?"

"Yes, you're doing very well. You used an interesting choice of words and I'm wondering if it was deliberate. No matter, it's a point we can come back to later; I don't want to distract you. Please continue."

"Okay, let me think about it some more. If I could have a coffee refill it would help my brain cells work faster."

Mwalimu refilled his coffee and the Salesman thought about ways he could draw a better analogy—how he could make a better connection between the hunting styles of African big cats and his own business development habits. He reviewed the major characteristics of the lion's style of hunting: Members of the pride drive prey toward concealed lionesses that then pounce on the prey to end the hunt.

In truth he had used a similar technique in the past to gain new business. He had played the role of the concealed lioness while his "pride" drove potential new business toward him. His pride did not growl or move on four feet; his pride was made up of anything or anyone that drove in prospects. For example, one member of the pride was any center of influence (COI) that referred business to him. In the Salesman's type of business these COIs were often attorneys, bankers and CPAs, but mostly they were his existing clients. When these COIs made a referral, they were literally driving business toward him like the lion's pride did in Tanganda.

Two days ago, when he met Mwalimu, he realized that he was not sufficiently nurturing the COIs that used to send business his way, nor was he cultivating new COIs. If he continued to neglect them, they would stop driving the clients toward him and he would have no hope of getting his lion's share of the business. His lesson about the lion's hunting style had re-emphasized the important role of COIs within his pride.

Another "member of his pride" was the limited amount of advertising he was already doing. These ads also drove business toward him. Yesterday the zebras reminded him of the importance of advertising and today the lions underscored the zebras' lesson. He was already committed to becoming more effective at delivering his message using thoughtful advertising. Now he better understood how his advertising fit into his pride.

Now his thoughts shifted. The rugged face of the lion that he had been seeing with his mind's eye slowly transformed into the handsome face of a cheetah. The cheetah's solitary hunting style is a 180-degree detour from the lion's team approach. Neither was necessarily better. They were just different. The Salesman had also used this technique to hunt for new business, but until today he had never stopped to think about the characteristics of cheetah-style business development. He turned the pages of his mental flip-chart to summarize the cheetah's style: the careful target selection, the patient but persistent stalking and the final dash; then he started making connections between the cheetah's behavior, the lion's behavior and his own behavior as a salesperson.

Target Selection: The cheetah selects a single animal as its target. There are times when the Salesman identified a specific target that he believed should have a need for his services. The target might be as specific as an individual person, business or organization. Such specific target selection has risks as well as rewards. If the target is selected correctly, then the chances are improved for a successful hunt. If the target selection is faulty, then the likelihood of success is remote. This rule applied equally to the cheetah and the Salesman.

This is a vastly different technique from lion-style hunting. Lions drive a large number of zebras toward their concealed partners, then they hope they can bring down at least one of the animals in the surprise attack. Lion-style business development works in a similar way. A large number of prospects are driven toward the Salesman by COIs, advertising, seminars and so on. Some of these prospects may have a high potential for conversion to clients, others may be clearly unqualified prospects that will never become clients. The Salesman must try to figuratively bring down at least one of the prospects that the pride drives toward him.

Stalking: The cheetah patiently, persistently and determinedly stalks its prey. The way that salespeople can stalk is by making regular, periodic, meaningful contact with the target prospect. Stalking is the important action bridge between identifying a specific target and obtaining a new client. This phase of the hunt must be meticulously implemented. If the stalking is done oafishly the target will get spooked and run away from the hunter at top speed. On the other hand, if the stalking is done with precision, the hunter is placed in a position that will improve the chances of success during the final dash.

If stalking is to be successful, it must persuade the target prospect that the salesperson has a solution to a problem that has not, or cannot, be solved by any of the competitors. If the prospect doesn't have a problem or a need, then the salesperson is not going to convert the target into a client. Often, however, the prospect has a need but just doesn't know it. Then it's the salesperson's job to make the prospect aware of the unknown need. Once the target prospect is aware of the need and has acknowledged that a solution must be found, the salesperson can offer his proposal for the solution. At this point the stalking is nearly finished.

Lions stalk with much less finesse. The cheetah delicately stalks a single animal using grace and precision. The lions try to create enough sound and fury to stampede a herd of animals into an ambush. When the Salesman is in his lion mode, he can't use finesse and precision. He has to appeal to the widest possible audience and hope that one or two would be interested enough to do business with him. Compared to cheetah mode, lion mode is crude but effective.

Final Dash: Stalking with perfect execution does not guarantee a successful hunt for a cheetah, a lion or a salesperson. The purpose of stalking is to put the hunter in a position that will increase the likelihood of success. Ultimately, the success or failure of the hunt is determined in the final dash. It is the breathtaking acceleration of the cheetah and the awesome ambush of the lion. For the salesperson, the final dash is that moment when he asks for the business.

Business Jungle Survival Skill:			
Hunting Styles	The Real Jungle		The Business Jungle
	Cheetah	Lion	Businessperson
Target Selection	A specific animal	A herd	*Lion mode:* COIs that can drive business in *Cheetah mode:* an individual person, business or organization
Stalking	Stealthy, patient, creeping up on the target	Create sound and fury, stampede the herd toward an ambush	*Lion mode:* ads, seminars, COIs *Cheetah mode:* Regular, frequent, meaningful contact with the target
Final Dash	70 mph sprint	Ambush from the bushes	*Lion & Cheetah mode:* natural conclusion to a conversation; seek agreement on what happens next and when

There cannot be a successful hunt if there is no final dash. The cheetah would starve if it never took the first stride in its burst of speed that catches the swift Thomson Gazelle. The time and energy spent on target selection and stalking is wasted. The cheetah will never have the satisfaction of feeling its jaws close on the throat of its prey if it doesn't make the final dash. The same law of the jungle is equally pertinent to the salesperson. If he doesn't *ask* for the business he won't *get* the business.

For cheetahs and lions, only one in four hunts will be successful. Unfortunately salespeople aren't so lucky; for them only about one in ten hunts will be successful, which makes the final dash even more meaningful.

Many salespeople like to refer to the final dash as "the close." They believe that the prospect must agree to buy immediately or the salesperson has failed. These people believe that the close should be as ferocious as it is in the real jungle. They refuse to take no for an answer and verbally assault the prospect until he reluctantly submits.

All of these notions are ludicrous. Salespeople who think this way are ignoring Mwalimu's advice that the laws of the jungle have a symbolic application in the Business Jungle. Hard closers are applying the law of the jungle too literally. In the Business Jungle, the final dash means reaching agreement with the prospect about what will happen next and when it will happen. To be sure, the lion and cheetah must "close" the first time or they go hungry. Because they only have one chance to close they do it with savage ferocity. Salespeople who adopt the same behavior will have the opposite effect—they will become extinct in the Business Jungle.

The Salesman thought he had a good grasp of these lessons. He appreciated the differences in the hunting styles and had made solid connections between the Business Jungle and real animal behavior. He understood why it was important for salespeople to be flexible enough to use either style of hunting for new business, and he had recalled times in the past when he had actually used both styles. However, he was not yet ready to share this knowledge with Mwalimu. She wouldn't consider the lesson complete until he could demonstrate his mastery of the "what," the "why" and the "how" of the subject.

The "what" of this lesson consists of the two styles of business development: lion-style and cheetah-style. The "why" is the advantage of using either style to successfully hunt for new business. The "how" of the lesson was less clear, like looking at a photographic slide that was out of focus. He had a general picture of the "how," but since Mwalimu would undoubtedly quiz him, he wanted to sharpen the focus until he understood the entire picture clearly.

How exactly should I employ these styles of hunting for new business? he asked himself. He began to ponder the answer to this question when a deep rumbling in his stomach reminded him that they hadn't eaten breakfast yet. It was always difficult for him to think on an empty stomach. A moment later, as if she had anticipated his hunger, Mwalimu handed him a bowl of dried fruit and grain which had been cooked for a few minutes in boiling water and sweetened with honey.

"Here you go Mwanfunzi. I've found that it's easier to fill your head with ideas after you first fill your stomach with food. Care for more coffee? There's a little bit left."

The Salesman nodded appreciatively and resumed turning the focus adjustment knob of his mental projector. He figured there were three "how's" he needed to bring into focus:

1. How to select a target
2. How to stalk a target
3. How to successfully conclude the hunt

Target selection is the first part of the hunt for new business. It is of vital importance. This part determines the ultimate outcome of the last part of the hunt so it must be done with utmost care. The Wicked Witch of the West could have been discussing target selection when she croaked at Dorothy, "These things must be done del-i-cate-ly."

If the delicate but vital process of target selection is the foundation of a successful hunt, then the foundation of target selection is laid within the business plan. The wildebeest and the hippo helped the Salesman to see that the foundation of the business plan was its definition of the market niche. Together these processes formed a business development pyramid. This pyramid, like a true pyramid, would topple over if it lacked a firm, wide base as its foundation. Target selection is the apex of the pyramid, definition of market niche is its base and the business plan is the connecting masonry.

When building the business development pyramid, target selection must be derived from the niche definition, not the other way around. If the pyramid attempted to define its market niche from its target selection, then it would be balanced on its apex, not its base. Sooner or later the inverted pyramid would topple over, perhaps crushing the salesperson under it. The Salesman wanted to give Mwalimu a specific example of this pyramidal process. He didn't have enough time to construct a thorough example, so he came up with a simple, but demonstrative, illustration:

Business Jungle Survival Skill:

Building the business development pyramid

Selection
Business Plan
Definition of Market Target

First, build a solid base by defining a market niche. His niche would consist of the charitable foundations of private hospitals and private universities in the 3 counties surrounding his office and having investment assets of $5 million or more. This was a good definition because it was *specific*.

Business Jungle Survival Skill:

A seven-step strategy for effective target selection

Lion mode:

Step 1: Write down the specific definition of your market niche from the Survival Tool on page 82.

Step 2: Write down the names of at least three COIs who could refer prospects from within your niche.

Step 3: Write down the names of at least three periodicals these prospects read for ideas and advice.

Step 4: Write down the title of at least one seminar you could present to these prospects.

Cheetah mode:

Step 5: Write down the specific definition of your market niche from the Survival Tool on page 82.

Step 6: Write the names, addresses and phone numbers of the top 10 individual prospects within your niche.

Step 7: Write down the date by which you will make contact with each of the 10 prospects.

Second, write a business plan that identifies the needs of the niche, identifies products and services which he can offer that will meet the needs, and identify a systematic approach to contacting prospects within the niche.

Third, select specific targets within the definition of the niche. Target selection will be partially determined by the mode of business development he is using, cheetah mode or lion mode. In lion mode, instead of selecting a target to stalk, he would focus on the members of the pride who could drive the business toward him. These pride members could be COIs, advertising or seminars. In this particular example, he would cultivate the accountants and attorneys who advise the foundations and the wealthy people who donate to them. His goal is to be at the top of the mind of a CPA or attorney when a foundation director asks them, "Do you know any good financial advisors?"

The Salesman would also place ads in the periodicals that foundation directors read for ideas and advice. Using the lessons learned from the zebras, his ads would offer solutions to challenges commonly encountered by foundations. The call to action would urge the readers to contact him. In other words, drive business toward him.

While in lion mode, his seminar strategy would focus on two fronts. First, he would offer to be a guest speaker at the regional conference sponsored by the professional association to which foundation directors belonged. Such a speaking engagement has some attractive benefits. He gets to be in front of a large number of prospects at one time and in one place and being in the position of "guest expert speaker" instantly raises his credibility. The second front would be to offer a seminar that the Salesman himself would sponsor and at which he would also be the guest speaker. He would advertise this seminar and also send invitations to prospects. Sponsoring such a seminar offers the same attractive benefits, but to a slightly lesser degree. That is because his stature may be slightly reduced by sponsoring his own seminar that is rather self-serving because the prospective attendees will be aware that the seminar is designed to be a business development tool. As an invited guest speaker at a professional conference, he has the added benefit of an unspoken, unofficial stamp of approval from the sponsoring organization, disclaimers from the sponsors notwithstanding.

Also, in this particular example, there is yet another member of the pride that can be very successful at driving business toward him. The decision-makers at foundations often belong to a professional organization. The boards of directors of these organizations sometimes give official endorsements to providers of products and services that are of interest to the organization's membership. If the Salesman could be anointed as the "Official

Financial Advisor of the Eastern Tanganda Foundation Directors Society," he would enjoy special access to members of the Society and receive a boost to his credibility. His endorsement, instead of being tacit, is now outright. Such endorsements can drive a lot of business toward him. However, because of the weight they carry, endorsements aren't easy to come by. They may require a substantial investment of time and money to obtain but may be worth the effort. The desired consequence of target selection while in lion mode is to build up the pride so that its members drive business to the Salesman. Then, when the prospects are in range, it is up to the Salesman to use his communication skills to uncover needs, create an awareness of needs, propose solutions, and finalize the interaction.

Target selection while in cheetah mode is somewhat simpler. Like the wild cheetah, the Salesman will personally select individual targets. He will then stalk the target with the same diligence, determination and patience exhibited by the cheetah he had observed stalking the gazelle. Remembering that target selection is derived from the definition of his market niche, he would only select individual targets that fit the definition. In this example his niche consisted of the local charitable foundations of private universities and hospitals with investment assets of $5 million or more. Any foundation that passed through those screens would be eligible to go on his target list, for example, John Q. Bigwig, Executive Director, Upper Crust University Foundation, assets $6.25 million. Any foundation that did not pass through the screens was eliminated from consideration as a prospective new customer.

Following this simple method of target selection would help the Salesman pinpoint his energy in a highly efficient manner and help him avoid the distraction of unproductive issues. He concluded that the "how" of target selection was now in much sharper focus.

He was so deeply lost in his thoughts of hunting in the Business Jungle that he failed to notice he had finished his coffee or that Mwalimu had cleaned up their few dishes and dismantled their simple camp. Gradually a feeling of discomfort seeped into his thoughts, discomfort caused by sitting too long on the fallen tree without moving. A basic law of human behavior is that the mind can only absorb as much as the buttocks can endure, and so, his reverie was broken for the moment.

The sun was well above the rim of the earth on the eastern horizon. The rich, damp, loamy smell of the river was carried on the gentle breeze; a couple of black and yellow swallowtail butterflies swirled around a sage blossom. It was going to be a glorious day to walk the remainder of their safari.

Business Jungle Survival Tool:

A six-step strategy for building your business development pyramid

Step 1: Draw a large pyramid on the flip-chart. Use the whole page. Divide the pyramid into five equal levels. Now, in the base of the pyramid write down the specific definition of your niche from the Survival Tool on page 82.

Step 2: On the next level up in the pyramid, write down the top three needs of the prospects within your niche.

Step 3: On the next level up in the pyramid, write down the top three products or services you offer that will meet the needs.

Step 4: On the next level up in the pyramid, identify a systematic approach to contacting the prospects within your niche (telemarketing, mail, advertising, seminars, other methods, or some combination). Write down the preferred method.

Step 5: On the top level of the pyramid, write down the names of the top prospects. In lion mode, write down the names of ten COIs, titles of seminars or types of media in which you can place ads. In cheetah mode, write down the names of 10 individuals you will personally contact.

Step 6: Finally, over the top of the pyramid, write down the date by which you will make contact with your top prospects.

"I think I'm forming some pretty good ideas, but they're like a steel ball in a pinball machine. They're ricocheting everywhere. I need to get the pinball machine under control before I try to tell you about them. It must be getting late; do we need to get started?"

Mwalimu glanced at the rising sun. "It's about 9:30 or 10:00. We'll probably get back to my *vijiji* by sundown, but you never know what might happen along the trail that could delay us. I think we should get started."

Ten minutes later, they had finished packing their things. When they walked away from their campsite, there was no trace of the sojourners. Even the campfire ashes had been disbursed so that they could work their way into the ground and enrich the soil. "I can tell that you're preoccupied with the lessons offered by Simba and the cheetah. You just keep thinking about them, and

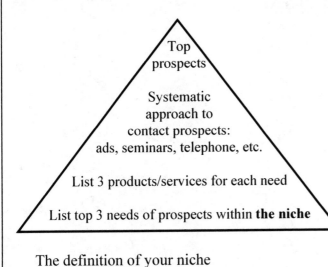

Business Jungle Survival Tool:

A six-step strategy for building your business development pyramid, this tool works well when you draw and write on a flip-chart. Date by which you will make contact: _____

Top prospects

Systematic approach to contact prospects: ads, seminars, telephone, etc.

List 3 products/services for each need

List top 3 needs of prospects within **the niche**

The definition of your niche

when you're ready we'll talk," Mwalimu remarked as they joined a different game trail, this one headed roughly northward.

"The first part of our safari today will follow the edge of the river, but after a kilometer or so we'll veer away from it. We'll eventually walk past my *vijiji* to the west and north of it, then circle back to the south to return to it."

The Salesman was a bit confused by Mwalimu's description of their route. "It sounds like we're going out of our way if we walk past the *vijiji* and then have to come back to it."

"That's true Mwan-funzi. But it isn't far and it will be worth the extra walking because I'm going to introduce you to a herd of elephants."

"You're going to introduce me to a whole herd of elephants, huh?" the Salesman shook his head in disbelief and smiled.

"Yes, and before we meet those elephants I suspect you will have the opportunity to learn from many other animals along the way," she smiled back at him.

Mwalimu led him along the trail at the edge of the river and quietly hummed another native tune while the Salesman returned to his contemplation of the "how's" of this lesson.

The Laws of the Business Jungle

15. Choose your hunting mode.

A lion can't hunt like a cheetah. Neither can a cheetah hunt like a lion. Businesspeople, however, can and should use both hunting styles.

Chapter Nine

CULTIVATING COFFEE AND CUSTOMERS

The first "how" of the lesson about lion- and cheetah-style prospecting had pertained to target selection. Now that this was clearer, the Salesman began to consider the second "how"—stalking. Stalking is the collective term that describes all of the action steps taken after the target has been identified. Its objective is to move the hunter closer to the target so that the hunter is in a more advantageous position from which to launch the final dash. How then, mused the Salesman, does a salesperson successfully stalk his target?

If the Salesman had had a dictionary in his backpack, he would have found that stalking is defined as "creeping upon stealthily." When Tanganda's predatory cats hunt for food, stalking is a perfect description. However the term has a sinister connotation when it is applied to people rather than cheetahs and lions. It was his strong belief that there should never be anything sinister about the sales process. The entire process must be conducted with dignity, respect and complete honesty. Prospects make positive buying decisions when they feel that they can trust the salesperson. The salesperson must maintain his integrity every single minute of every single day or he will never earn the prospect's trust, nor will he deserve it. Lions are successful hunters because they hide in the bushes and ambush their prey. Professional salespeople must never hide in the bushes. Integrity demands that they must always be up front with both customers and prospects. In the Business Jungle, salespeople who ambush their prospects may find enough to eat, but they will not prosper and sooner or later they will become extinct.

Consequently, the Salesman felt that the analogy about stalking didn't connect to the Business Jungle. Still, he felt there was a valuable lesson here. He mentioned his misgivings to Mwalimu.

"You make a very good point Mwanfunzi," she replied to his concern. "Your misgiving is soundly based. Let's think about this dilemma and see if we can't resolve it."

She thought for a moment as she watched the darting flight path of a river swallow, and then asked him, "Just what do you consider stalking to be. I mean in the Business Jungle, not in the real jungle."

"When I think of stalking as it applies to the Business Jungle I think of an adversarial process—sort of salesperson vs. prospect. I think of a salesperson who's motivated solely by what's in it for him. I think of shady, shoddy sales practices, too."

"Such as?"

"Such as sending junk mail that's vague, ambiguous or misleading. Or how about inconvenient telephone calls at dinnertime with promises of goods or services that can't be delivered. The high-pressure sales pitches that browbeat and badger a prospect are worst of all."

"Tell me Mwanfunzi, how do you think prospects feel about being stalked?"

"I'm sure they don't appreciate it."

"Okay. Let's figure out what we've discovered so far." Mwalimu paused briefly and then said, "It sounds to me that if a salesperson were too literal in the application of the analogy about stalking it would result in an unsuccessful hunt for new business. Do you agree?"

"Yes," the Salesman nodded, "because prospects and customers don't like being stalked."

"I'm sure you're right about that. Salespeople will eventually face extinction if they stalk their prey in the Business Jungle in the same manner that cheetahs and lions stalk their prey in the real jungle. We agree that while stalking is effective here in Tanganda, it is a problematic process in the Business Jungle. Nevertheless, there must be a series of action steps between target selection and the final dash. Consider this Mwanfunzi, cultivation is an alternative term with a much more positive but equally appropriate meaning.

"To cultivate," she explained, "means to foster the growth of something, to nurture it. For example, a coffee tree is cultivated from a seedling into a sapling and is finally nurtured into a mature, bean-producing tree."

The Salesman was vigorously nodding his head as Mwalimu explained the definition. "Oh yeah," he said. "I like this way of putting it. When I think of this definition as it applies to my business, I think of cultivating new relationships from prospects, into customers and finally into mature, referral-producing relationships."

"Exactly, Mwanfunzi. You make a much stronger connection to the Business Jungle when you stop stalking and start cultivating."

One of the success keys to stalking is not to stalk at all but to cultivate. The Salesman's mental picture about this "how" was getting less fuzzy but was still a long way from clear; he needed to crank the focus control knob some more. Now the obvious question becomes *how does one cultivate successfully?*

"I'm not very good at growing things," the Salesman shrugged. "Once I tried growing a small vegetable garden; I managed to harvest a half-dozen tomatoes. With all the time and money I spent on that stupid garden, I figure each tomato cost about $9! But I like this idea of cultivating new customers. Since I'm basically clueless about the practice of cultivation maybe you can clue me in."

"I would be happy to do that Mwanfunzi. Cultivation is one topic I happen to know a little bit about."

"Why doesn't that surprise me, Mwalimu? I think you know about a lot of topics."

"Thank you for the compliment, but I think you're giving me too much credit. Anyway, anything I do know is thanks to the teachers I've had in my life."

"Like who? Who have been your teachers?"

"Oh, maybe we can talk about that later. Right now let's talk about the basics of cultivation and how they apply to the Business Jungle."

She ducked my questions again. She's never going to tell me about her past, he thought.

"Okay," he said aloud. "Talk to me about cultivation."

"The form of cultivation I'm most familiar with pertains to coffee, so I'll use that as my frame of reference. I'll make you an expert at growing coffee trees. How's that sound?"

"Sounds good to me. Who knows, if I get tired of the investment business maybe I can start a coffee plantation."

The trail they were following began to curve away from the river. Before it disappeared behind them, they paused for a last look down at the serene waters. A small herd of hippos was busy filling their huge mouths full of grass and bellowing their odd grunts in contentment. As they stood on the edge of the gorge, Mwalimu explained that the process of cultivation is not a complicated one. The hallmarks of success are consistency and a systematic approach.

Proper cultivation is accomplished by systematically completing a series of steps. If any of these steps are taken out of order or omitted, the process won't work.

She listed the steps:

>Step 1: Prepare the soil.
>
>Step 2: Plant the seedling.
>
>Step 3: Feed and water regularly.
>
>Step 4: Prune the branches as needed.
>
>Step 5: Harvest the beans.

"Systematic completion of these steps is mandatory," she continued. "Think about it, common sense dictates that nothing will be accomplished if the soil is prepared after the seedling is planted. It's impossible to prune the branches until after the food and water has been applied so that the seedling is able to produce the branches that need to be pruned. Consistency is just as important as the systematic approach.

"Every step needs to be done with great consistency. The soil must first be prepared to receive the seedling, and then the soil must be tended consistently by pulling weeds and controlling dangerous pests that make a home in the dirt. Without the consistent application of food and water the young seedling will fail to thrive and will eventually die. Less frequently, but no less consistently, the growing tree must be pruned. This selective removal of certain branches helps to channel the tree's energy in the most productive way. Dead or stunted branches are cut off so that the tree wastes no energy trying to revitalize them. Even some living branches are trimmed to shape the tree's growth.

"The orchardist's goal when the first seedling is planted is to someday harvest the beans. A consistent application of a systematic approach to cultivating the coffee tree enhances the probability of reaping a hard-won crop but doesn't guarantee it. The orchardist cannot control or influence everything in the cultivation process. Drought, pestilence, fire, storms and other assorted natural phenomena can have an effect on the bounty of the trees, ranging from reducing the yield to wiping out the entire crop.

"Assuming that nature's forces don't undo the orchardist's best efforts, the time will come when that which was sown is ready for harvest. The quantity and the quality of the beans plucked from the branches of the coffee trees are the prize for a job well done."

Mwalimu concluded, "But the grower knows that the timing of the harvest must be exact. If the beans are picked too early or too late their flavor will be disappointing, and all the work will have been for naught."

"Okay, now I have a better understanding about what happens before the coffee ends up in the espresso machine. But how does all that relate to the Business Jungle?" asked a puzzled Salesman.

"There is a very strong correlation, Mwanfunzi. I know you can make the connections. Indeed, you've already made one."

"Yeah, I said that cultivating a prospect into a mature, referral-producing relationship was better than stalking. I can see that connection clearly, but I'm having a little trouble connecting this other stuff. How the heck does pruning dead limbs off coffee trees have any connection to what I do inside my office on the 23rd floor of a downtown skyscraper?"

Mwalimu wore an unmistakable look of exasperation.

"Mwanfunzi, that 'other stuff' has everything to do with your business, including the part about pruning. You're just going to have to figure this out for yourself. I suggest you give it some more thought and tell me what you come up with."

She turned her back on the river and stalked off down the trail.

"Whoa! Wait a minute!" he called after her. The Salesman trotted down the trail to catch up with her. "I didn't mean to make you angry with me."

"I'm not angry with you, Mwanfunzi, but your behavior is very disappointing. You have shown me how insightful you can be and I have raised the bar. Then you simply stop trying to learn. The connections between cultivating coffee and customers are not that difficult to ferret out. You are happy to swim on the surface of this lesson, yet you have the ability to dive deeply into it. It disappoints me when you do that. I consider it a waste of your intellect because I know you can do better."

Like a naughty 4th grader who had just been chewed out by his teacher, he looked at her sheepishly and said, "I'm sorry."

She stopped and looked at him, fixing him with a piercing stare. "Do you think that Simba can survive out here if he doesn't give survival his utmost effort every day?"

"No, I don't suppose he can," the Salesman replied, scuffing the dirt with his right foot.

"Hear me well, Mwanfunzi. You won't survive in the Business Jungle if you don't exert the utmost effort every day. If I'm hard on you when I think you're slacking off, that's why."

"Okay, I'll try harder. I'll mull this over until I figure it out."

"That's the spirit, Mwanfunzi! If you get stuck, I'll help you get unstuck. But I'm simply not going to make the connections for you in this lesson. That's your job. Now, let's get moving."

Teacher and student resumed walking and left the Masara River behind them. The warming sun on the right side of the Salesman's body helped to relieve a few of the aches he'd gotten from sleeping on the ground. He couldn't remember the last time he'd slept on the ground, and this morning his body was letting him know that it preferred something softer.

During the safari he had learned to watch his step on the uneven game trails, watch the abundant life all around him, and also to meditate upon the lessons he learned from Mwalimu and the animals. Now he turned inward once again to find the connections with cultivation that had eluded him and earned Mwalimu's chagrin.

He replayed Mwalimu's explanation of the cultivation process and considered how each of the steps might apply to the Business Jungle. Mwalimu had said that the first step in growing a coffee tree was to prepare the soil. He thought: *What does that have to do with me? What does it have to do with cultivating a new customer?*

A coffee tree can only grow if the proper steps are taken in the proper order and if the grower is consistent in her approach. The same can be said for cultivating new customers. If preparing the soil is the first step in growing a coffee tree, then the equivalent action for a businessperson is to formulate a written plan for a business development campaign. Any initiative that is undertaken in the Business Jungle should be thoroughly planned. There is no doubt that the ability to improvise is a valued trait, but it should be done infrequently and only when prior planning isn't working as intended. The process of cultivating new customers cannot be improvised, haphazard or left to chance.

Like any business plan, a business development plan needs to be SMART about setting goals and objectives—*specific, measurable, attainable, relevant, time-bound*. In addition to developing this plan, the businessperson must also till the soil by doing things like drafting letters that will be sent, selecting the design and layout for ads that will be purchased, even writing the script for the telephone calls that will be made. A retailer might spade the soil by selecting merchandise that will be promoted, deciding on price points that will be offered, designing displays that will be built, and more. Other types of businesses will have other ways to prepare the soil.

The Salesman felt that he had finally soldered a solid connection into place. In the Business Jungle, preparing the soil was equivalent to completing all of the preplanning that must be done before a business development campaign can begin.

The focus knob made another click in his quest for clarity of understanding about this lesson. *What was the next step?* he asked himself. *Oh yeah, plant the seedling.*

When the soil has been sufficiently prepared to receive it, the coffee grower will plant the seedling. The bean of the coffee tree is also its seed. While most of the beans are harvested and roasted to supply the world with its daily caffeine fix, some of the beans are used for their true purpose—to grow more coffee trees.

These beans are carefully sprouted and closely tended until they are a couple of inches tall and have sprouted a couple of glossy green leaves. Then the seedlings are ready to be planted. The planting of seedlings in the ground instead of seeds has a couple of advantages. First, the seedling has a higher rate of survival and can become a producing tree faster. Second, when the seeds are sprouted they can be in a closely controlled and monitored atmosphere instead of being subjected to the caprices of nature.

What then does it mean to plant a seedling in the Business Jungle? After the soil has been prepared by planning the business development campaign then the seedling needs to be planted. The seedling...the seedling...the seedling *what?* The Salesman was stuck.

What is the seedling? He was tempted to ask Mwalimu to help him get unstuck but he resisted. He wanted to get himself unstuck. If he found that he was totally stumped then he would ask Mwalimu for help.

Okay, it shouldn't be this hard. Think about it from a different angle...what would I do next? What's the next step I would take in the business development process?

Then he had a blinding flash of the obvious; the seedling was the first actual contact with the target prospect. Planting the seedling was making that contact. Planting the seedling meant calling the prospect and actually having a conversation, not merely leaving a message. It meant mailing a letter that the prospect opens and reads rather than consigns to the junk mail graveyard. It meant placing an ad in a newspaper or magazine that catches a reader's eye. Maybe that reader even tears out the ad and saves it for reference.

The focus was becoming ever more clear.

If the seedling is never planted it can never grow and mature. If the first contact is never made with the prospect, he will never become a customer. This seemed so obvious, yet many salespeople hesitated to initiate that first contact, mostly out of fear of rejection. If they simply understood this lesson about cultivation they would understand the inanity of their hesitation. In the Business Jungle, failing to plant seedlings by making actual contact with prospects will result in a stagnant business. No new business means starvation. Starvation means extinction. The Salesman decided he would become a regular Johnny Appleseed in the Business Jungle.

Now that he'd solved the riddle of naming the seedling, he figured that the next step, feeding and watering, was easy. Once a seedling is planted in the orchard it doesn't explode out of the ground into a full-grown tree, Jack and the Beanstalk notwithstanding. In order to grow, the seedling must be fed and watered, but an occasional dumping of fertilizer or a periodic dousing of water just won't work. These things need to be done at the right times and in the right amounts, consistently.

In the Business Jungle, prospects don't turn into customers overnight. They need to be fed and watered, too. The Salesman made an immediate connection with this part of the process and the way it worked. In his business, prospects rarely made affirmative buying decisions after only one contact. It was necessary to stay in regular, periodic contact with each of them. Often this contact can be made by sending letters, making follow-up phone calls, extending invitations to seminars and the like. These activities represented the feeding and watering of his prospects.

For retail businesses that relied primarily on advertising to garner new customers, the feeding and watering process is similar. The prospects need to be fed and watered with a regular diet of ads placed in the correct media so that they will be seen, read and recognized. This diet should be supplemented with an active public relations campaign so that the retailers name is in front of the prospect frequently.

Feeding and watering a coffee tree needs to be done at the right time and in the right amount. Watering during a rainfall is a waste of resources. Dripping a thimbleful of water during a drought is a waste of time. Neither the timing nor the amount is appropriate and the seedling won't grow. Prospects and existing customers need to receive the right amount of food and water at the right time. If the prospect receives too much information she may become overwhelmed and postpone her decision-making while she processes it all. This paralysis of analysis can even lead to an indefinite postponement of a decision.

Similarly, if the prospect is contacted too often, the salesperson runs the risk of appearing over anxious to make a sale. Prospects may feel antagonistic toward a salesperson that is too anxious, and they are not likely to buy if they feel antagonized. They are not likely to buy if they think the salesperson is concerned with his agenda rather than their own. To appear overanxious sends the message that the salesperson is unconcerned about the prospect's needs and that is a very bad message indeed. Too little contact is just as bad as too much contact. A long period between contacts sends the message that the salesperson doesn't care enough about the prospect to persist in earning her business. During the long intervals between contacts, a window is open for the competition to move in and snatch the prospect away.

There is no generic formula to follow in the feeding and watering of prospects. There is no magic number of contacts to make, no perfect interval between contacts. The final formula for how often and how much is ultimately determined by the characteristics of the target prospect and the product or service that the salesperson is offering. But once the optimal formula is determined, it must be used consistently to achieve lush, full growth of the seedling.

The focus knob on the mental projector made another quarter turn.

Earlier the Salesman had provoked Mwalimu's ire by making a flippant remark about pruning a coffee tree. When he made that unfortunate remark this concept of cultivation and how it applied to the Business Jungle was new to him; he hadn't had time to let it sink in. Now that he had gotten used to the idea, it was easier to deduce the applications and connections that he had not seen before. Like an apprentice electrician he was learning to make the connections faster and more securely. So it was with pruning.

Pruning in an orchard is done to control and direct the growth of a coffee tree. In the Business Jungle, pruning is done for the same purpose—to control and direct the growth of a business. Pruning is the process of cutting away the prospects and the customers who can't or won't buy.

When a campaign is undertaken to cultivate new business it should be based on realistic expectations. The reality is that only about one in ten prospects is going to turn into a customer. This means that nine out of ten prospects will suck up time, energy and money and not give any business in return. It's incumbent on the salesperson to quickly recognize those nine who won't or can't buy and take the pruning shears to them. They're dead wood, cut them out! Bring up the prospect list on the computer, select those names and hit the delete key.

Not only should some prospects feel the sharp edges of the pruning shears, so should some existing customers. Sure, many customers will do repeat business, but a lot of them, for a variety of reasons, only do business once and nothing more. These are one-shot customers and they pose a potentially serious survival threat to a salesperson. They insidiously siphon off the salesperson's resources. Why? Because many businesspeople believe that all customers are created equal. Such altruistic balderdash has no place in the savage environment of the Business Jungle.

Customers are hard to come by, *very* hard to come by. Each one that is acquired is precious. Once a customer has been acquired it is understandable that a salesperson wants to hang on tightly to the prize and never let go. While this is understandable, it is a misguided emotional attachment. The salesperson desperately clings to the belief that if a customer bought something in the past that the same customer is bound to buy again in the future. So the salesperson continues to send letters, make phone calls or buy ads to convince that same customer to buy again. But one-shot customers are never going to buy again and all those resources are going to waste.

Another reason to prune is that existing customers require a certain amount of maintenance and record keeping on the part of the business. In some cases this maintenance can be a gargantuan task. This is especially true of brokerage firms, banks, insurance companies, credit card issuers and lots of others. It costs the same amount of resources (both human and monetary) to prepare and send a statement to a $1 million customer as it does a $1,000 customer. Add to that the cost of record keeping and reporting required by regulatory agencies and pretty soon the cost of customer maintenance adds up to real money. One-shot customers suck up these resources like a galactic black hole and never produce revenue to help offset the cost of their upkeep.

When salespeople have the mistaken belief that customers who bought once will inevitably buy again, they are lulled into a false sense of security by having hundreds (or thousands or even millions) of customers on the books. With this false sense of security comes complacency. The salesperson thinks: *Hey, I got a jillion customers! I must be doing great!* Complacency is the seed of disaster.

Here's a wake-up call for businesspeople everywhere: The health of the business is not determined by how many customers you have; it's determined by how many you are getting. If new customers are not constantly added, then not only will the business stop growing, it will slowly but surely shrivel and die. It will become a smorgasbord for hyenas.

In this savage environment that is the Business Jungle, prospects that can't or won't buy and one-shot customers need to be hacked away. If they aren't pruned they will wear down a business and drain its resources like a leech drains the blood of its host.

The Salesman was satisfied that he had made yet another connection between Tangandan coffee and the Business Jungle. His mind raced to make the final connection in the process of cultivating new customers: the harvest.

The harvest is the realization of the grower's dream. When the beans are plucked from the branches of the coffee tree they are a tangible reward for all the work that went on before. Coffee growers know that not every seedling in the orchard will grow up to produce beans for the harvest. Of the trees that do produce beans, some will be abundant, others sparse.

Mwalimu had explained to him that the timing of the harvest must be calculated exactly; picking the beans must happen at the peak of their readiness. An inexperienced grower may pick the beans too soon or wait too long in an attempt to capture the last few moments of ripening only to let the beans become overripe. Either way, the grower has failed to maximize the results of the harvest.

Coffee beans are the seeds of the coffee tree. Most of the beans are harvested, but some of the beans are reserved for their original purpose. It is from these seeds that the seedlings are coaxed. Then when the seedlings are judged to be strong enough, they are planted in the orchard and the cycle of cultivation is renewed.

The Salesman perceived that for the salesperson, the harvest is the reward for a carefully planned, consistently applied business development campaign. The harvest is the moment when the prospect is converted into a customer. The satisfaction that is felt when the prospect says "I've decided to do business with you" is the coffee bean being plucked from the tree. Not every prospect will grow into a customer; some clients will bring lots of business, others only a little.

Timing of the harvest is just as important in the Business Jungle. If the salesperson tries to make the harvest too soon, the prospect will not be ready to make a decision. The salesperson runs the risk that the prospect will be lost forever because she feels she is being pushed into something. If the salesperson waits too long, a competitor might get through the fence surrounding the orchard and steal the low-hanging fruit cultivated by the salesperson. Either option is an undesirable outcome.

To renew the cycle of cultivation some of the harvest is used to sprout new seedlings. This means that customers must be asked for referrals. When a referral is received the name of the new prospect is added to the business development campaign list and the cultivation process begins anew.

The Salesman felt a gentle tap on his arm. He blinked, looked to his left and saw that Mwalimu was looking at him questioningly.

"We've been walking for close to an hour and you haven't said a thing. I thought I should bring you back to the real world for a minute," she said.

"An hour! I had no idea, sorry. I've had a lot to think about, want to hear?"

"Talk to me, Mwanfunzi. Talk to me!"

The trail had just entered into a large grove of acacia trees. It was pleasantly cool in the dappled shade of the grove. They sat in the grass at the side of the trail and the Salesman began.

"When I started to think through the entire hunting process it was not completely clear to me at first. But now I've reviewed each of the steps: target selection, stalking/cultivating and the final dash. I discovered that I didn't like to use the term 'stalking,' but I like very much to use the term 'cultivating.' I've thought about the styles of hunting and the cultivation of coffee and I've made connections between them and the Business Jungle."

Then the Salesman gave Mwalimu a long, rambling explanation of this thought process. As he was reaching the end of his explanation, he had begun talking about the final harvest but was stopped in mid-sentence by the roar of a lion that sounded nearby.

Mwalimu turned to him and said excitedly, "I think we found the lion that woke you up last night. Let's take a closer look, shall we?" She headed off in the direction from which the roar came.

"Uh, wait a minute, Mwalimu!" the Salesman yelled after her, a note of alarm in his voice. "Do you think it's wise to barge in on a hungry lion who's busy devouring whatever he caught?"

Mwalimu stopped, turned and walked back to where the Salesman was rooted to the trail. "No, it's not wise to *barge in* as you said. We need to be cautious about how we approach Simba and he won't be concerned about us. I want you to remember a couple of things. First, whatever Simba caught is probably mostly eaten by now. Second, after Simba feasts he is too gorged to be very active; he'll be too lethargic to care about us. Third, we'll keep some distance between us and at no time will we get between he and his kill. Is that clear?"

"Yeah, it's all clear. I'm just not sure how safe it is." He had an obvious look of concern on his face.

"I've told you that I don't fear Simba, but I do respect him a great deal. If you do what I say, we're in no danger. Besides, this may be your only chance to photograph Simba; he is one of the Big Five you know," she reminded him. She folded her arms and said, "It's up to you. If you don't want to go, we won't."

The Salesman remained rooted in the trail mulling over the situation. He trusted Mwalimu but he also had a strong sense of self-preservation. Thinking back to his indecision about even agreeing to this safari in the first place, he knew that he had come to another line drawn in the sand by his comfort level. Did he have the guts to cross over this one, too?

"Okay," he finally agreed. "Let's go. But only long enough for a quick photo and then we're outta there!"

Mwalimu was beaming. "An excellent choice Mwanfunzi. Not because you chose to take a picture of Simba, but because you hit the wall of your comfort level and pushed beyond it. If you can condition yourself to recognize that when you hesitate it's because you've reached the upper limit of your comfort zone and then automatically push back against that wall, you will continually push your comfort level higher and higher. That is something to be proud of!"

"Yes, but it's very hard to do. Every time I feel uncomfortable about doing something you want me to go ahead and do it for no other reason than because it has made me uncomfortable in the first place. My nature, and most all human nature, is to shrink away from that which makes you uncomfortable," replied the Salesman.

"That is very true. People don't like to be uncomfortable; we know that. Wouldn't you agree, though, that every time you do push against the walls raised by your comfort level, you always ultimately overcome the short period of discomfort? On the other side of that discomfort your comfort level has been reset at a new, higher level. The prior event which had caused you discomfort will not cause it again. For example, you had to overcome your discomfort to undertake this safari. The next time you have the opportunity to go on safari it will be easy for you to agree because you have reset your comfort level at a higher level. Does that make sense?"

"Yes, intellectually I agree. Emotionally, I still don't like to feel uncomfortable."

"You never will like it. Just recognize what the feeling means and try to use it to your advantage."

Mwalimu walked again in the direction from which the roar had come. A short distance off the trail, they came to the edge of a small clearing surrounded by tall bushes and shaded by an enormous acacia tree. Peering through the bushes into the clearing they could see a lion, four lionesses and a couple of cubs lying in the shade. In the center of the clearing were the remains of a zebra that had almost been completely consumed.

The Salesman carefully raised his camera, adjusted the focus and exposure and took several quick photographs. He signaled to Mwalimu that he was finished and ready to leave; they silently retraced their steps to the trail.

"Now that we're back I'm glad we took that little detour," the Salesman smiled weakly and sighed. "I guess I reset my comfort level again. The next time you want to go look at some lions up close I suppose I'll be more willing. I hope those photos turn out okay. Now, where was I before we got off-track?"

"You were telling me how both the big cats' lessons of hunting and the lesson about coffee cultivation can apply to the Business Jungle," prompted Mwalimu.

"Oh yes, now I remember. I was just starting to explain about harvesting when the lion roared. The timing of that roar was perfect because it brings us right back to lions and cheetahs; the final dash is the same thing in their world as the harvest is to coffee cultivation. They are synonymous activities."

"Tell me more about the final dash," Mwalimu asked.

"Just as the harvest is the culmination and final payoff of the grower's efforts, the final dash is the culmination of the hunt. Hunger or satiation will be decided upon the final moment. Earlier it occurred to me that many salespeople are doing the final dash all wrong."

"Why is that Mwanfunzi?"

"Because they try too hard. They're too aggressive."

"And why is that a problem?" Mwalimu asked.

"Because people who don't want to be stalked don't want a pushy, hard closer in their face."

"We've already agreed that makes sense. So how should the final dash be done?"

"I think the final dash should be a simple and natural conclusion to a discussion about a prospect's needs. The objective is not necessarily to get the business but rather to agree on what the next steps are going to be and when they will be taken. A lot of times the next step *is* to do business but not always."

Mwalimu listened closely and nodded.

"What salespeople need to realize is that it is okay if the prospect doesn't agree to do business immediately. The important thing is that the prospect agrees that there will be a next step and agrees on when the step will take place. This agreement must be reached before the conversation ends. In this way the sales process stays alive and actively moving forward," he concluded with a confident nod of his head.

Mwalimu nodded back. "Excellent, Mwanfunzi. Your thoughts are well reasoned and equally well spoken."

The Salesman gave a small sigh of relief.

Mwalimu continued, "When you talked about the final dash just now you said it should be the natural conclusion to a conversation about a prospect's needs. This is an important point."

"I'm glad you agree, Mwalimu. But what about the final step in the cultivation process—asking for referrals?"

"Yes, an important part of the process. It's how you re-seed your orchard—in other words, how you use existing customers to sprout new customers. Salespeople don't earn the right to ask for or receive a referral based upon performing a transaction. Salespeople receive referrals when they have built a relationship with the customer."

"And how would you advise me to build these relationships?" the Salesman inquired.

"Ah, that is the reason I want you to visit the elephants."

"I'm anxious to see them. Shall we go?"

He stood up and offered his hand to Mwalimu who was still sitting in the grass at the side of the trail. She brushed a few twigs from her *kanzu*, picked a burr off her shawl and remarked, "I'm sure we'll have the opportunity to learn a few more laws of the jungle before we get to the elephant herd. This acacia grove looks like an excellent habitat for one of our most unusual animals."

BUSINESS JUNGLE SURVIVAL SKILL: CULTIVATING COFFEE AND CUSTOMERS

	COFFEE TREE	BUSINESS JUNGLE
	Prepare the soil	Plan the campaign
	Plant the seedling	Make the first contact
	Water and feed	Regular, consistent contact
	Remove dead wood, control and direct the tree's growth	Remove clients or prospects who can't or won't buy
	Pick the beans at the peak of their ripeness	Agree on the next steps and when they will be taken
	Plant some of the beans that were harvested	Ask for referrals

The Laws of the Business Jungle

16. Cultivate, don't stalk.

Cultivate new business using a disciplined, systematic and consistent approach.

Chapter Ten

In the Company of Giraffes

Acacia trees are quintessentially African. Just as coconut palms are the signature tree of tropical beaches, the acacia is the signature tree of Africa, and photos of the African savannah invariably include them. They aren't especially tall, and the tops of the acacias are incredibly flat, as if a giant hedge trimmer had been at work shaping them. Their flat canopies spread wide, creating great swaths of welcome shade. The trees' branches and leaves are small, giving it a delicate and wispy look, but the look is deceiving because the tree is remarkably durable and tough. The 2-inch thorns that grow on its branches are evidence of that.

Mwalimu and the Salesman walked deeper into the acacia grove. The Salesman was startled to see a small mouse impaled on one of these thorns.

"What happened to that poor little guy?" he wondered out loud.

"We have a small predatory bird that lives around here called a kite. When it makes a kill, it hangs the prey on an acacia thorn for a while. Later, he will come back to eat the mouse, but in the meantime it will be safe from scavengers. Now I have a question for you, actually I have a couple of questions," added Mwalimu.

"I hope I have a couple of answers."

She continued, "When we were having our coffee this morning and talking about hunting styles, I noticed that you made an interesting choice of words. At the time I didn't want to distract you by asking about it but now I do."

"What was it that I said?"

"You said that when a lion and a cheetah are hunting it's analogous to when a salesperson is prospecting for new business."

"Yes. So..."

"Why did you say salesperson? If I remember correctly, you've always used the term businessperson. Why the change? Was it deliberate?"

"Actually it was deliberate. See, I think that the hunting lessons I learned are most applicable to salespeople."

Mwalimu considered this for a moment. "What you're implying is that business-people are not salespeople."

"No, that's not exactly what I meant. I think that all salespeople are businesspeople but not all businesspeople are salespeople. The guy who does my dry cleaning is a great example. It's a small business so the owner works the counter, operates that conveyor belt thing where he hangs all the clothes and puts plastic bags over my clean suits," explained the Salesman.

"Am I to understand that you consider this man a businessperson but not a salesperson?"

"Right. This guy does a good job cleaning clothes, but he's probably never made a sales call in his life!" he declared derisively.

"Why do you do business with him?"

"He does a good job, he has reasonable prices and his store is in a very convenient location. Probably his location is the biggest reason; it has nothing to do with his ability—or lack of ability—as a salesperson."

"I see," Mwalimu said thoughtfully. "It sounds like you made a unilateral buying decision; this dry cleaner met your I&A expectations and your need for a convenient location. You didn't need to be sold anything, so the owner didn't need to have any sales skills."

"That's exactly right, Mwalimu."

"What would happen, Mwanfunzi, if you found that a competing dry cleaner had opened for business while you were here in Tanganda? Let's say that the new dry cleaner did the same quality of work, was even more convenient and charged the same price or even a little bit more. Would you continue to do business with your current dry cleaner?"

The Salesman didn't hesitate. "Nope!" he replied simply.

"If you did take your business elsewhere, what do you think your former dry cleaner would do?"

"Do?" The Salesman wore a puzzled frown. "I don't think he'd do anything. I doubt that he would even notice that I wasn't coming in anymore. You sure are interested in my dry cleaner! How come?"

"Because he proves your point that not all businesspeople are salespeople. I agree with your point, and I will carry it a step further. All businesspeople *must* be salespeople no matter what business they are in. There is no business big or small that couldn't do better if it would always be selling."

"I certainly agree with what you just said, and I'll carry it *even further*. Businesspeople who do not become salespeople will, sooner or later, lose the battle for survival in the Business Jungle."

"We are thinking as one mind on this issue, Mwanfunzi. It's a shame that more businesspeople don't understand this law of the Business Jungle."

Mwalimu placed a hand on his arm indicating that he should slow down. She pointed to the side of the trail where a herd of zebras enjoyed the comfortable shade of the acacias.

A couple of zebras raised their heads to assess the potential threat from the two humans, decided they were harmless and resumed their grazing.

"A while ago, when you talked about pruning, you made some strong statements that some of your colleagues might not understand or agree with. Let's talk about that."

"Okay, let's. Basically I said that some clients and prospects turn into deadwood and could be cut off."

"Well, Mwanfunzi, you won't win any awards for diplomacy."

"I guess I was being rather blunt, but I didn't realize how important pruning is until I thought about it in terms of cultivation."

"It is important, that is why I want to discuss it thoroughly. For you, or any businessperson for that matter, to recognize the truth of this lesson

---

Business Jungle Survival Skill:

This is a four-step pruning strategy. Prospects are kept in the orchard for no more than three weeks.

Step 1 / Day 1 / Call: Attempt to plant a seedling by telephoning the prospect. If no contact is made—in other words, you did not have a conversation with the prospect—leave a message. Schedule your contact management system to bring up the prospect's name again in two days.

Step 2 / Day 3 / Mail: If the prospect hasn't returned your call, send a letter asking the prospect to call you. Remember, you must offer the prospect a good reason to call you back. Schedule your contact manager to bring up the prospect's name again in 10 days.

Step 3 / Day 13 / Call: If the prospect hasn't called in response to your letter, call the prospect again. If no contact is made, leave another message. Schedule your contact manager to bring up the prospect's name again in eight days.

Step 4 / Day 21 / Prune: If the prospect still hasn't returned your call, she isn't interested. Delete the prospect's name from the prospect list.

demonstrates enlightened thinking. Not many businesspeople have the wisdom to understand this.

"A coffee grower must make sure that he trims the correct branches at the correct time, or he could actually stunt the tree's growth. Businesspeople have to be equally careful. Tell me when you propose to prune your own clients and prospects without stunting your business."

"Well, to be honest, I guess hadn't really thought about that part."

"The 'when' of this lesson must be very clear. Let me fill in the blanks for you."

Mwalimu explained that prospects fall into two categories. The first is the "unable to contact" category. This category requires careful contact management so that regular attempts are made to contact the prospect and the results are tracked. For example, some businesspeople will use a call-mail-call strategy. Here's how it works: When a prospect's name is received, a telephone call is attempted within 24 hours. If no contact is actually made then a message is left. If the call had not been returned within two days, a letter is mailed which offers an appointment and asks the prospect to call to confirm the appointment. If no return call is received within 10 days, the businessperson makes another attempt at calling by telephone. If no contact is actually made on this second attempt then a message is left again. If the prospect doesn't return the second call within eight days, his name is pruned from the list of prospects. Mwalimu reminded him of the cultivation process again. If the seedling is never planted, in other words if no contact is actually made, then the tree can't grow and there is no point in having the prospect's name cluttering up the prospect lists. Bottom line: call-mail-call-prune.

The second of the two categories of prospects is the "unwilling to agree" category. This represents prospects with whom contact has been made but the prospect has made no agreement on what steps will be taken next. If such an agreement cannot be reached then the sales process has been effectively quashed and the prospect can be pruned.

As Mwalimu related this to the Salesman his face registered a look of alarm. "Wait a minute! You are absolutely correct when you say some of my colleagues won't understand this. You just said that we should deliberately shorten our prospects lists; that's blasphemy for a lot of sales, er, I mean, *business*people!"

Mwalimu held up her hands, "It's not as simple as what I just said. Let me finish and maybe I'll resolve your concern."

She went on to explain a huge caveat to her previous statement. Before a prospect is labeled "unwilling to agree" and pruned away, the businessperson must first be confident that he has uncovered all of the prospect's needs and has offered a solution to those needs that meets the prospect's requirements. If the prospect is unwilling to agree that the solution meets a need or if he agrees that it meets a need but is unwilling to agree to the next steps, then the prospect can be safely pruned.

"Does that resolve your concern, Mwanfunzi?"

"Yes it helps, thank you. When you view it in those terms it is very logical and sensible. I'm still a little anxious about how to prune my existing clients. Will you tell me your thoughts on that please?"

"The only clients that should be pruned are one-shot clients; the clients who will not or cannot buy any more goods or services." Mwalimu explained that there was a huge caveat here, too. In this case, the businessperson must be confident that he has attempted to cross-sell/up-sell the clients. Perhaps the only way to gain this confidence is to have a rigorous approach to the cross-selling/up-selling activities.

Mwalimu peered at him and asked, "Do you understand what I mean by cross-sell/up-sell? I want to make sure we understand each other clearly."

"Yes, I understand those terms. Here's what they mean to me. I define 'cross-selling' as selling additional products or services to the same client. These additional things would be different from the product or service they already have. For example, the client already owns product A, and they buy some of product B. That's cross-selling. I define 'up-selling' as selling more of the same product or service to the client. In other words, the client owns some of product A and then buys more of product A. That's 'up-selling.'"

"Good Mwanfunzi. Those are clear definitions and the same way I would define the terms."

Similar to cultivating a prospect into a new client, the broadening and deepening of relationships with existing clients is an exacting process. When a client makes a positive buying decision it is because she believes the businessperson can solve a need. The goal of cross-selling/up-selling is to uncover additional needs, propose additional solutions and gain additional business. During the course of the cross/up-sell activities the businessperson will discover some clients who have no additional needs. In a needs-based selling technique the absence of needs means that no further business can be transacted. Those clients can be safely pruned.

Pruning existing clients must be done with sensitivity. It would be folly to tell the clients that they must purchase more goods or services or they will face ostracism. Clients deserve being treated with dignity and respect. This must be balanced with the businessperson's need to allocate resources in the most effective manner. The reality is that one-shot clients cannot be allocated the same amount of time as clients who regularly do repeat business. But it will behoove the businessperson to determine a graceful way to perform the pruning.

As Mwalimu spoke the Salesman nodded his head in comprehension and agreement. Then Mwalimu reminded him that from the standpoint of expending resources effectively, it is much cheaper to obtain additional business from existing clients than it is to obtain new business from new clients. That's another very good reason to be diligent about cross-selling/up-selling activities.

The trail was climbing steadily. Now they reached the top of a low hill. On the other side of this small summit the ground sloped downward into a large bowl-shaped shallow valley. They were standing at a point on the rim of the bowl and saw that the bottom of the bowl was filled with more acacia trees and a smattering of flame trees.

What the Salesman saw next took his breath away.

"Oh my gosh! That looks like a scene out of that dinosaur movie; what was it called… Jurassic something-or-other?"

Among the trees was a small herd of eight or ten giraffes. The foliage obscured their large bodies, but their graceful long necks soared to the tops of the trees and sometimes beyond the treetops. They were reminiscent of brontosaurs as they grazed on the leaves of the topmost branches.

Mwalimu agreed. "Yes, they do look prehistoric, don't they? I think it's their great height that gives them that aura. At just under 20 feet tall they are the world's tallest mammals. Not only does their height give them the ability to reach the tenderest leaves of the acacia tree, it also gives them a great view since they also have the best vision of any big mammal."

The Salesman watched them with a mixture of awe and wonder. The giraffes stretched their necks to their full length and plucked the leaves with their 17-inch tongues. Some pulled a branch into their mouths and with a quick twist of the head they stripped off all the leaves, including the 2-inch thorns.

Mwalimu appeared to be mesmerized by the giraffes, too.

"I never get tired of watching them. It seems that they have always awed people. Cave paintings in northern Africa dating to prehistoric times frequently included giraffes."

From the other side of the little valley they heard the unmistakable rumble of a Land Rover. It made its way down to the bottom of the bowl and stopped so the visitors inside could get a better view of the giraffes. One of the curious youngsters in the herd began to wander toward the vehicle to get a better look at the odd contraption. An older male giraffe, probably the dominant bull, noticed that the youngster was headed toward the Land Rover and apparently decided it was getting too close. The bull quickly strode over to the youngster and using his neck like a hook he herded the youngster away from the car.

"Did you see that, Mwalimu? I swear that big giraffe went over there to keep the little one out of trouble."

"You may be right, Mwanfunzi. A giraffe herd is a very close community, more so than many other kinds of herds but not as much as elephants. Elephants have the strongest sense of community among all the herds of Africa. It has been my observation that the giraffes do seem to watch out for each other."

At that moment the engine of the Land Rover fired up and the excited tourists went back the way they came, destined no doubt for another appointment with some other Tangandan wildlife. They watched the car disappear over the rim of the bowl and Mwalimu remarked to the Salesman, "What we just observed when the bull giraffe went to the assistance of the young giraffe reminded me of something my friend the General said. The third of his three keys to success is to care about the people you lead. The bull is the leader of the giraffe herd. He showed that he cared about a member of his herd by keeping the youngster away from a potentially dangerous situation."

"I can see why you were reminded of that. You know what? The General's third key and our observation of the giraffes are the basis for another law of the Business Jungle."

"What might that law be, Mwanfunzi?"

"It's a law about how to manage people, how to lead a team."

Within the Business Jungle there is room for both managers and leaders. Businesspeople can survive in the Business Jungle as managers. However, to flourish in the

Business Jungle a manager must not merely manage, *he must lead*. Managers who are unwilling or unable to be leaders will still have an important role in the Business Jungle, but their role is much different than a leader's role. Although businesspeople can survive as managers in the Business Jungle, business enterprises that have only managers will not survive. Business enterprises must have both managers and leaders.

A person becomes a manager when someone simply bestows the title, but *leader* is not a title to be handed out by the human resources department. Leadership is a quality in a person's character. It is a philosophy of doing, a style. A person becomes a leader when the members of his team come to appreciate and value his influence and when the team members themselves recognize that he is not a manager but a true leader. Because co-workers bestow the label of leader, it is a precious label indeed, and one that is difficult to win.

One of the important qualities of leadership is to care about the people who are the followers. The interlude with the giraffes provided a fine example of how to demonstrate a caring attitude. Leaders, giraffe or human, feel compelled to watch out for younger or less-experienced co-workers. They feel obligated to steer them away from potentially dangerous situations, just like the giraffe bull did for the younger giraffe. A leader is characterized by six important qualities:

1. Allows the team to struggle
2. Communicates frequently
3. Encourages participative decision-making
4. Instills a vision
5. Fosters two-way communication
6. Cares about the people being led

1. Allows the team to struggle:

A good leader is able to quickly size up a situation facing a co-worker to determine if it could be dangerous to the co-worker's career or to the business enterprise itself, or if it is merely a difficult situation. This is a distinction of some consequence; if the situation is only difficult then the co-worker should be encouraged to tackle it and struggle with it. However, if it is truly a dangerous situation then the leader needs to work quickly to help steer the co-worker to safety.

Allowing a co-worker to struggle with a difficult situation is the mark of a leader, as is allowing a co-worker to make a mistake. These same qualities of leadership promote the growth of co-workers so that they become more valuable members of their team. Such leadership communicates to the co-worker that he is trusted and has the confidence of the leader. It creates an environment in which the co-worker feels the leader will support him. Within this kind of environment an interesting phenomenon occurs. The more often a co-worker is allowed to persevere through those uncomfortable, difficult, trying situations, the less often they seem to occur. Before long the co-worker can recognize potentially dangerous situations himself and avoid them on his own.

In short, these qualities of leadership say to the co-worker, "I care about you."

Managers who are not leaders do not allow co-workers to struggle with a difficult situation. Instead the manager rushes in and takes over, precluding any learning, growth or development of the co-worker. Worse yet, it sends a negative message that says, "I have no confidence in you, and I really don't trust you. It is not okay for you to make a mistake, so I'm going to barge in and take over to make sure this is done right." When a manager sends this message she will never be a leader because she's also saying, "I don't care about you." In order to be a leader there must be someone to follow, but no one wants to follow a leader who does not care about people.

"I guess what I'm saying Mwalimu, is that in the real jungle bull giraffes look out for younger giraffes. In the Business Jungle leaders need to look out for their co-workers."

Mwalimu made no response. From the far away look in her eyes she was obviously deep in her own thoughts. This time it was the Salesman's turn to wait patiently while

Mwalimu finished her thoughts. He heard the giraffes rustling the leaves and branches of the acacia trees and turned his gaze toward where they were browsing. Then Mwalimu spoke.

"You've reminded me of a conversation I had a long time ago. It's a conversation I'll never forget, although I haven't thought about it for a year or so, until now.

"I once asked someone to tell me her definition of a leader. She said, 'A leader is someone I would follow, if for no other reason than out of sheer curiosity, to see where she would lead me.'

"That depth of loyalty and dedication would never be accorded to a manager that didn't care about her team and her co-workers. That is the kind of leader I aspire to be. I should think it a worthy goal of any businessperson."

Now Mwalimu also turned her gaze toward the giraffes and together they watched a scene that would have looked much the same a million years ago.

"Well Mwanfunzi," she said at length, "it seems that we were lucky to be in the company of these giraffes. They showed you some things that are germane to your own jungle. I liked what you said about the essential leadership quality of caring. You gave some good examples of how to care about co-workers: allow them to make mistakes, empower them to struggle with and learn from tough situations, and protect them from dangerous situations. Can you tell me other ways that a leader can show he cares about those whom he leads?"

The Salesman scratched his head and then swatted at a fly that was buzzing around one of his ears.

2. Communicates frequently:

"Communication comes to mind," he replied, "frequent, thorough, unambiguous communication. When a leader communicates in this manner he's saying, 'I respect you.'"

"What do you mean by 'communication,' communication about what? Can you give me an example? And what does it all have to do with respect?" she quizzed him.

"How about this example: A leader needs to communicate expectations about each co-worker's contribution to the overall team effort. After each co-worker knows what's expected for their individual performance, then the leader needs to regularly tell them how they are measuring up. The mere fact of engaging in such communication demonstrates the leader's respect for the co-workers."

"Good example, Mwanfunzi. In what other ways does a leader show he cares?"

3. Encourages participative decision-making:

"Participation is another thing that comes to mind," he replied.

"Participation?"

"Yes. A leader invites co-workers to participate in the decisions that affect the team. I know you're going to ask me for an example, so I've got one for you. When the team sets a goal, all the team members should participate in the goal-setting process. When the whole team sets the goal, good things happen. The team members become invested in the goal itself and assume ownership of it. As a result they will probably strive harder to achieve it.

"Another good thing that happens is that the team will probably have higher expectations of itself and thereby set more aggressive goals. Often managers who impose goals on teams underestimate the team's abilities and set goals too low."

"What I hear you saying is that when a manager imposes a goal he sends a message that says, 'I have a low opinion of your capabilities, and I don't value your input.' But a leader who invites participation sends the opposite message. Is that right? Did I understand you correctly?"

"That's what I'm saying, and I know which person I would rather follow."

"Yes, the choice becomes rather obvious doesn't it? What else can you tell me, Mwanfunzi?"

The Salesman scratched his head again. "I'm sure there are other things, I just can't come up with them right now. I think I need to give my brain a break."

"I have a couple of thoughts that you haven't mentioned. Would you like to hear them?"

"Of course I would!"

"Let's resume our walk and I'll tell you along the way."

Mwalimu led them down the hill and across the floor of the little valley. They gave the giraffes a wide berth so as not to disturb them. Crossing the floor of the valley they came upon a stream that tumbled down into the valley in a series of small cascades on their right. The stream meandered through the bottom of the valley and flowed out of it through a cleft in the hills to their left. It was a simple matter to cross the stream by walking across a dry sandbar and then stepping across the water on several large flat stones. Mwalimu explained that this was the same stream they had crossed the day before when she had given him his sandals. Not too far beyond the hills to the left, the stream merged with the Masara River.

After rock-hopping across the stream they climbed up the slope on the far side of the valley. They weaved their way through the acacia trees making sure to avoid the stabbing thorns.

"Mwalimu how do the giraffes eat this stuff? Don't the thorns perforate their insides?"

"No Mwanfunzi, thorns are not a problem for them. Their saliva is extraordinarily thick and gluey. It helps protect that long throat and stomach."

"Oh Mwalimu, that's pretty gross!"

"You asked..."

"I know, I know. I'll have to remember to bring up the topic of giraffe saliva the next time I'm at a fancy business lunch."

He laughed out loud as he visualized himself in an elegant restaurant; he leans over to his lunch companion and says: *"The sauce on your salmon reminds me of a story about giraffe saliva. Did I tell you about the time I went to Tanganda.... "* He thought this would be enormously funny.

The Salesman's humorous visualization faded, and he said to Mwalimu, "Okay, back to the lesson at hand. You said you had a couple of thoughts..."

4. Instills a vision:

"Yes, just two more things for you to consider on this topic of caring leadership. Managers tell co-workers what to do. Some people may need this kind of instruction, especially new and inexperienced co-workers. However, a lot of people, especially seasoned co-workers, find this approach condescending at best, belittling and demeaning at worst. Leaders instill a vision of the team's mission; they set the context by explaining the big picture and then define the team's role within it. This is no easy task, but once it is accomplished the leader gets out of the way and lets the team get to work on achieving its mission.

"This is caring leadership at its best, Mwanfunzi. The co-workers feel that they are valued contributors to the overall goals of the team and the company. They feel included because they understand what the vision is and how their efforts can help achieve it. No longer do they feel like mindless cogs in a massive machine that grinds out a product or a service. Who knows, they might even become *inspired* about their work!"

"Wow! That's the kind of a leader I would want to work for. Maybe I can even be that kind of leader some day."

"You will be, Mwanfunzi. You will be."

"I appreciate your confidence in me; I wish I shared it."

"Whether you realize it or not, you are already more confident in yourself than when I met you two days ago."

"Well, maybe I am feeling a little more confident..."

When they emerged from the valley of the giraffes they entered a broad arid pan of dried and cracked earth. This was the bottom of a shallow lake, and although the rainy season had been over for only a short time, the soil had absorbed most of the water and the sun had evaporated the rest. Now the lake was as dry as a chalkboard. It was hot on the lakebed. There was no shade to protect them; the sun's solar strength beat on them fiercely from above and then reflected off the baked earth to strike them from below. The Salesman was very uncomfortable; Mwalimu didn't seem to notice.

They walked in silence as they crossed the lakebed. The Salesman was much relieved to see that the lakebed was only about 100 meters wide. On the other side, where the far shore would be during the rainy season, was the welcoming shade of more acacia trees and an ancient baobab tree that towered over the surrounding acacias. A few minutes later they had traversed the dry lakebed and entered the shade.

"Can we take a little break? It was awfully warm out there. Just looking at a picture of a dry lake makes me hot. Actually walking across one is as unpleasant as I had expected." He wiped his sweating forehead with his shirtsleeve and took long swallows from his water gourd.

"That was the hottest part of our trip. It's not quite noon. It'll be even hotter on the dry lake in mid-afternoon. I wish you could see this lake in the rainy season. The rainfall transforms that little wasteland into a wondrous oasis that teems with life. Animals come from all around to drink here. Thousands of birds—flamingoes, ibises, egrets, and herons—all flock to the lake where they wade in the shallow water and gorge themselves on shrimp."

"Looking at the lakebed now it's hard to believe anything would come here on purpose. I guess I'll just have to come back here in the rainy season, won't I? Hey, wait a minute, you never told me your second thought."

5. Fosters two-way communication:

"While you're cooling down, I'll tell you that leaders foster two-way communication, while managers communicate in one direction only—from themselves down to the co-workers. Let me give you an example of two-way communication from my personal experience. I once knew a manager that many people considered a leader. This manager, or leader, always made sure that her team members knew exactly what she expected of their performance at work. She and her team members would collaborate and jointly set performance objectives for the team and each member. Then she would meet regularly with each individual to give them very specific feedback about their performance."

"It sounds to me like this leader was just doing employee performance reviews. I'll grant you that she was doing it the way a caring leader would do it, but it's still just a performance review. There's really nothing groundbreaking about that," shrugged the Salesman.

"Here's the groundbreaking part, at least according to a lot of her co-workers and colleagues. After she reviewed each employee's performance, she asked the employee to review her performance. She had even created a formalized process by which the employee could write this performance review."

"Wait a minute," the Salesman interrupted, "you mean like a performance review *in reverse*?"

"Exactly."

"Oh, man...that's a gutsy move."

"Maybe. At first her team members were taken aback. Employees don't normally review the performance of their boss, except maybe in the form of derogatory comments, complaints and other moaning. At first they were reluctant to do it at all because they were afraid that legitimate criticism might be held against them."

"It's understandable that they might be suspicious. What did this manager, er, leader do to get around this suspicion?"

"She suggested that they submit their evaluations anonymously. For a while that's what a lot of them did, but they quickly realized that she was serious about truly wanting to receive their feedback, and they no longer needed the cloak of anonymity."

"Did she really do anything with this feedback or was it all just a big show to impress her team?"

"I can see that you're cynical about management's motives, Mwanfunzi! In this case, the leader really did do something. She made it a part of her own personal development plan to work on those areas in which her team said she needed to improve. Then she really worked on those areas, told her team what she was doing and then ultimately asked them if she was showing any improvement."

"That's unbelievable, Mwalimu."

"No, that's leadership. That's two-way communication at work. It's another example of caring leadership."

"You said this example was from your personal experience. Did you work for this manager?"

"I guess you could say that. You sound surprised; why?"

"Well, ummm, I don't know," he stammered. "I guess I'm surprised that you worked anywhere. You haven't been too talkative about your past."

She laughed. "I haven't spent my entire life in my *vijiji*, you know."

"No, I don't know. Where have you been? Where was this job you had, and what did you do?"

"We have so much to do on this safari that we don't have time for you to know my life's story. Besides, it's irrelevant to our purpose."

"Mwalimu you're killin' me! I'm dying to know about your life and you won't tell me anything!"

"I'm flattered, but I told you, it's irrelevant. You're forgetting what the Thomson Gazelle taught you about focus. What you need to focus on right now is to learn from these animals the things that will help you to grow your business. My background is simply a distraction, an unproductive issue you should avoid."

She pierced him with her bright, dark eyes as she spoke. It was abundantly clear that there would be no further discussion about this topic. Then she smiled and said, "I really am flattered by your curiosity. Thank you. Maybe there will be a time when your learning about my background will not be a distraction, and then I will be happy to answer your questions. For now we'd better get back on the trail."

The Laws of the Business Jungle

17. Businessperson = Salesperson

All businesspeople *must* be salespeople no matter what business they are in. There is no business big or small that couldn't do better if everyone in it would always be selling.

18. Prune away clients and prospects.

One-shot clients and prospects who are unwilling or unable to buy will drain your resources and create a false sense of security. They must be pruned away.

19. Care about the people you lead.

Caring leaders interact with their co-workers in a way that makes the co-worker feel he is valued. Co-workers who feel valued by their leader will be inspired about their work.

Chapter Eleven

POACHERS

Mwalimu and the Salesman followed the trail to the base of the ancient baobab tree. The tree was many hundreds of years old and its base was so huge that it would take ten people holding hands with arms extended to encircle it. Dozens of weaverbirds had decorated its limbs with their pendulous nests and they hung like elongated teardrops woven of grass. The trail forked once it reached the baobab. The right fork ran northwards and the left veered sharply left to the west. The western ground rose steeply toward a range of hills that were two or three hundred meters high. Mwalimu paused for a moment as if she were considering which path to take. It was the first time since they began the safari that she had hesitated about which way to go.

"What's the matter; we aren't lost, are we?"

The Salesman trusted Mwalimu completely but his greatest fear was getting lost in the expanse of the Tangandan plains. He had asked the question half jokingly but he had portrayed a sense of concern.

"Of course we're not lost! I've walked this trail more times than I can remember. Every time I reach this spot I take a moment to offer a silent greeting to this baobab tree that is the guardian of the trail and ask his permission to pass. I'm also considering if we have time to take a detour on the left fork up into those hills; if we do, we're almost sure to see some rhinos."

She glanced up to check the sun's position. "We should have time. Let's go find a rhinoceros."

With that they turned left and struck out for the hills. Soon the trail began to gain elevation. It became steeper and rockier as they climbed. They negotiated a series of switchbacks and reached the summit of the first rank of hills. Between these hills and the next rank, which was still higher, there was an almost level bench of ground.

Mwalimu paused at the first summit to look back down on the plains below. At the foot of the hills, she saw the dry lakebed they had crossed. Turning to the right, she looked toward the valley of the giraffes and beyond that the gorge of the Masara River was at the edge of her vision. The Salesman continued along the path while she enjoyed the view, but he soon came to an abrupt and surprised halt. There was a man with a rifle over his shoulder with his back toward the Salesman standing on the path ahead. The man's attention was centered on two rhinos grazing alongside the trail.

The Salesman's mind raced as he tried to analyze the situation before him. He had heard stories about well-armed and vicious poachers who took enormous risks to illegally kill endangered and protected rhinos. The poachers stood to reap rich rewards when they sold certain parts of the rhino in clandestine Eastern markets. Indeed the payoffs were so rich that some of the rangers charged with enforcing antipoaching laws had been killed in action, murdered because they stood between the rhinos and the poachers.

Is this a good guy or a bad guy? Does he know I'm behind him? What's he doing here? What am I doing here? And what do I do now? The Salesman's thoughts came fast and furiously.

The rifleman continued to watch the rhinos.

Good, he doesn't seem to know I'm here. Maybe I can quietly go back the way I came.

At that instant he heard soft footsteps coming along the path behind him.

Oh no, do poachers work in pairs!?

He slowly turned to look behind him and saw Mwalimu marching up the trail oblivious of the rifleman blocking the trail ahead. He started to raise a finger to his lips to signal her to be quiet. As he did her face broke into one of her dazzling grins and she called out, "I see you found a rhino. No, *two* rhinos. Wonderful!"

The rifleman would have to be stone-deaf not to hear that! The Salesman spun around to look back up the path where the rifleman stood.

Sure enough, the rifleman had turned around when he heard the unexpected voices. There was a startled look on his face. The rifle was now off his shoulder and in his hands, casually pointed at the ground. The Salesman's stomach was just beginning to feel queasy and he cast his eyes about looking for a place to dive for cover if the rifleman started shooting. Mwalimu didn't hesitate and continued to walk up the path. She looked past the Salesman and shouted out, "Is that you Benjamin? Benjamin Batwani?"

The rifleman replied uncertainly, "Yes, I'm Benjamin..." Then a smile of recognition spread across his face. "Oh, it's you Mwalimu! *Habari* Mwalimu! How are you?"

The rifleman visibly relaxed. He swung the gun back over his shoulder and he began to walk toward them. Mwalimu brushed past the Salesman and walked up the trail to meet Benjamin. They embraced and began talking rapidly in Swahili. The Salesman let out a long sigh of relief. He noticed that he was trembling slightly, an aftereffect of the injection of adrenalin his body had given him. He moved off the path and sat down on a large rock in the shade of a tree.

Mwalimu and Benjamin continued to chat in Swahili for a few minutes. The Salesman overheard their conversation but he didn't understand a word. From what he could hear and see, it appeared that they were old friends who hadn't seen each other in a while and were catching up on all the recent news. Mwalimu waved to the Salesman to come over and join them.

"Mwanfunzi, this is Benjamin. He grew up in my *vijiji*, and now he's a ranger with the National Wildlife Protection Service. Everyone in the *vijiji* is very proud of the job Benjamin is doing. It's a difficult and dangerous job, but it's a vital and honorable occupation. I've asked him to tell you about it."

The Salesman was further relieved to hear that Benjamin was one of the good guys after all. He extended his hand and said, "It's nice to meet you, Benjamin. I'm glad you're a ranger, not a poacher. When I first saw you on the path I wasn't sure which side you were on, and I was very nervous."

"It's nice to meet you, too. I'm sorry if I made you nervous. I was a bit startled when I first saw you. I never know where or when a poacher might show up so I have to be cautious all the time." Benjamin spoke perfect English with a trace of a British accent.

"So tell me, what are you doing out here?"

"No doubt you noticed the pair of rhinos over there. Well, those are *my* rhinos," he replied, an obvious note of pride in his voice.

"What do you mean they're *your* rhinos?"

"My job is to stay with this pair 24 hours a day. I am their guardian angel; their personal body guard. I follow them wherever they may choose to roam."

"You mean you follow them everywhere? You sleep out here with them?"

"Yes, exactly. I work for three days straight, then I have the rest of the week off. We have Ranger outposts scattered around the area, and I keep in touch with them by radio so they know where I am. They keep me supplied with the things I need, and at the end of my shift, they bring out one of my partners to begin his watch. The rhinos are guarded 365 days a year, 24 hours a day."

"That's amazing! Why do they need armed guards anyway?"

"Unfortunately there aren't many rhinos left. In 1970 there were 65,000 black rhinos on the African continent. Not a very big number given the size of the habitat. Today there are fewer than 2,400 rhinos. Most of them live in Tanganda and Tanzania. The few that are left are at the top of the poachers' hit list. This species is so endangered that it would quickly become extinct at the hands of poachers. That's why my job was created; we rangers protect the rhinos from the poachers' bullets."

The Salesman was impressed. "That's an extraordinary commitment of manpower and resources. It would never happen in the USA."

Mwalimu broke in, "Extraordinary times call for extraordinary commitments. Fortunately, our government has the foresight to understand how important the country's wildlife resources really are. They place a high value on the wildlife and protecting it is a high priority."

"I still don't understand exactly why the poachers are so interested in the rhinos. What's the attraction?"

Benjamin pointed to the pair of rhinos munching away on the grass. "When you look at a rhino what do you see as its most prominent feature?"

The Salesman turned to observe the rhinos. If the giraffes with their long necks are graceful reminders of prehistoric times, rhinos are evidence that not all dinosaurs died out millions of years ago. To the Salesman, rhinos appeared to be the armored truck of Tangandan wildlife. They're almost the size of a real armored truck; the average rhino is 12 feet long, six feet tall at the shoulder and weighs a petite ton and a half. Their thick gray skin hangs in great sheets of armor, and the massive stumps that are their legs are able to propel them at up to 30 miles per hour.

The most prominent feature is that for which it is named: "rhinoceros" is Latin for nose horn. Actually it is a double horn made of tightly woven and compressed hair. The horn stands nearly 2 feet high and is anchored in the bone of the skull.

"To me, the thing that distinguishes the rhino is its horn, of course," the Salesman finally answered.

"Exactly," acknowledged Benjamin. "And the horn is the prize that the poachers seek."

"What on earth for? What does a person do with a rhino horn?"

"Use it for better sex."

The Salesman's jaw dropped. "I beg your pardon?"

"The horns are ground up into powder and then sent to China, India and other places in Asia where it has long been used as an aphrodisiac," explained Benjamin with a stern look on his face.

Incredulous, the Salesman shook his head. "You mean to tell me that poachers will kill a 3,000 pound animal just to get a few pounds of its horn!? And they are willing to exterminate an entire species so a few people can spice up their sex lives?"

"That's what it comes down to. Hard to believe, but easy to understand because the powdered horn commands a very high price."

The Salesman leaned toward the ranger and asked in a low voice, "Does it really work Benjamin? I would never, ever buy it, but I'm sorta curious."

Benjamin smiled. "Sorry, I wouldn't know. But an awful lot of people in Asia think that it works, and they're willing to pay a lot of money to get it."

"The high-risk, high-reward crime of poaching is a capital offense in Tanganda," explained Mwalimu, "and the enforcement of the laws is taken very seriously. Benjamin and all of his fellow rangers are authorized to use deadly force as necessary. They can shoot to kill any poacher they catch in the act of committing the crime; they don't even have to shout a warning before they pull the trigger. Should a poacher survive an encounter with a ranger and then be convicted of poaching, he'll spend the rest of his life in a Tangandan prison.

"Despite the risk, poachers use all manner of high-tech equipment to give them an edge over the rangers. The poachers have airplanes, helicopters, high-powered automatic weapons, night-vision goggles, and sophisticated communication systems at their command. Unfortunately the rangers aren't as well equipped. Although the government recognizes the importance of this law enforcement effort, it doesn't have the financing to equip the rangers as well as the criminals equip themselves. For example, not all rangers have rifles. Some have handguns; others have shotguns. The rangers are usually on foot, although some have bicycles. They are simply outgunned by the poachers."

Benjamin's face was a mixture of sadness, frustration and anger. "It's such a shame," he said. "We're slowly losing the battle with the poachers, not because we lack the commitment or skills, but because we lack the equipment."

The Salesman nodded his head in silent agreement, sharing Benjamin's emotions. Then he remembered the third of the General's three keys to leadership success: use the best equipment to execute your plan. The rangers were a harsh example of what happens if you fail to do that.

"Well, Benjamin, it was very nice to see you again. My mwanfunzi and I have a long way to go this afternoon. This side trip to see your rhinos has cost us some time, but it was time well spent. Now we must be going," said Mwalimu, embracing him again.

"It was nice to see you too Mwalimu. Say hello to everyone in the *vijiji* for me."

Benjamin turned to the Salesman. "You're a lucky man to be on safari with Mwalimu. Whatever the reason you began this safari, Mwalimu will help you find answers. There's a lot more to her than meets the eye. A number of years ago I went on a safari with her and it helped me to see that this would be my life's work and career."

"Thanks Benjamin. I've already learned a lot with her help. Say, do you mind if I take a picture of you with your rhinos? I'm attempting to get the Big Five on film."

After the Salesman took his photos Mwalimu led them away along the path, skirting the rhinos. When they were out of earshot of Benjamin, the Salesman said, "I didn't want to say this in front of Benjamin because I didn't want to appear negative, but I was thinking of the General's keys to leadership and wishing that Benjamin's bosses would understand the wisdom of those keys. If they did they wouldn't have such a problem now."

"You're correct, of course. As a matter of fact I've asked the General to share his keys to leadership with Benjamin's superiors and he's agreed to do it later this year."

"I didn't understand that you had a *personal* relationship with the General. How do you know him?"

"Irrelevant distraction, Mwanfunzi. Let's focus on the business lesson you've just had, okay?"

The trail they were following came to another fork. Mwalimu selected the right tine, which descended sinuously to the plains below and ultimately rejoined the original trail they had been traveling. The trails steepness and rockiness required them to concentrate on where they were putting their feet, and neither one said much until they once more stood on the familiar plains. Then the Salesman spoke.

"Okay, back to business. I think I already described the business lesson. The situation facing the rangers has occurred largely because they don't have the best equipment."

"That's true, Mwanfunzi. We are on this safari to help you solve your own challenges. How does the sad plight of the rhino in Tanganda apply to your business in the USA? I can assure you that there *is* a lesson that does apply to your Business Jungle. What do you think it is?"

In the Salesman's world of investing, quick reliable access to information has an importance that cannot be overemphasized. If one stockbroker can't provide the access that the customer expects, the customer will go to a broker who can. Providing the information the customer demands means making use of the best equipment and technology. The broker with the best equipment will attract and retain the most customers.

And so it goes with almost any business. A long-distance telephone service must have fast, reliable switching equipment because the customers won't be satisfied with slow connections. A tax preparer must have software that contains the most recent tax law changes or customers might overpay their taxes. A retailer must have products on hand that are included in whatever the current trend happens to be. If a clothing store were to offer bell-bottomed jeans when the trend called for straight-legged pants, the store would suffer the consequences.

The lesson of the rhinos has become a Law of the Business Jungle: If you don't have the best equipment then you will be outgunned by the competition, and the competition will start poaching your customers.

"Good work, Mwanfunzi. You had a bit of a shaky start, but in the end you once again analyzed a jungle lesson, and you saw how to use the lesson to write a new law of the Business Jungle," Mwalimu replied with satisfaction. Then she added, "I think however that this law is one that is likely to be disobeyed."

"Thanks for the compliment, Mwalimu," said the Salesman, pleased with himself. "I agree with your assessment of the potential for disobedience of this law, and here's why. At the intellectual level, most business people understand that if your customer wants to hire someone to dig a hole, you can't show up with a teaspoon while your competition shows up with a backhoe. At the gut level, businesspeople also realize that having the best equipment often requires substantial investments of capital. Because of the capital cost involved, many business people will try to get by more cheaply and in this way they violate this law of the Business Jungle."

Mwalimu concurred, "Yes, this law, of all the Business Jungle laws, will cost the most in dollars and cents if a businessperson abides by it. But consider this… the laws of the Business Jungle contain the same conundrum as any of the laws of man. If you break the law but don't get caught, has a violation really been committed? We debate this constantly; you ignore the parking meter because you don't have the right change and, besides, you'll only be gone for five minutes anyway. You take the risk that the traffic cop won't be patrolling your stretch of the avenue and you won't get a ticket. If you get back to your car and drive away before the traffic cop comes by, have you committed a violation?

"Sometimes the risk pays off and you don't get caught. What if the traffic cop comes by in three minutes while you're still involved in your five-minute errand? You probably slap yourself in the forehead, hard, and mumble to yourself: 'Why didn't I obey that law? Why did I take the risk? I wasn't willing to spend a dime, and now I have to pay $25.00!'

"The answer to this rhetorical question is, of course, obvious. You took the risk because you thought you could get away with it, and then when you don't, your hindsight is always 20/20. If only our foresight was so acute!"

She paused briefly, took a deep breath and continued. "So what does this have to do with anything? If a businessperson fails to obey this law of the Business Jungle and use the best equipment, she's saying to herself: 'I'll take the risk because I really don't think I'm going to get caught.' Maybe she won't, but maybe she will. Every businessperson needs to decide how much business risk she is willing to take. A person with a high tolerance for risk will only obey a few of the laws of the Business Jungle or none at all. A person with a low tolerance for risk will obey every one with great diligence. Every person in business today needs to decide where they stand on the business risk spectrum."

Mwalimu finished her sermon and looked at the Salesman apologetically. "Sorry, I got a bit philosophical and long-winded there."

"Not at all! You have a way of putting these things into perspective. Take my situation for instance. While I'm here in Tanganda discovering all of these really cool lessons and laws, I naturally plan to follow them all. When I get back to the reality of my office, or as time passes and memory fades, I'll probably be less diligent about obeying them. At least I'll know that I'm taking a risk by choosing not to obey, and I'll be making a fully informed decision about the risk I'm taking. Hopefully I won't get caught. If I do, I won't whine about it or berate myself because I did it with my eyes wide open."

"Here in Tanganda we have a saying that not even the giraffe with his long neck and sharp eyes can see the future. Since we can't see the future we must be sure that we do see reality. From what you've just said I know you're a realist; don't forget that, Mwanfunzi."

"No ma'am!"

The sun was scribing its perfect arc across the sky and had passed its zenith. Mwalimu suggested that they snack on the dried fruit and meat in their packs as they walked, instead of stopping to eat lunch. Now that they were again walking on the flat plains and were regularly cooled by the shade of the trees, it was much easier to make their way. The Salesman's muscles were by now warmed up and comfortably stretched. The minor discomfort of his earlier aches and pains had vanished, and he quickly agreed to Mwalimu's suggestion. Since this was the final day of his safari he wanted to take every opportunity to observe the wildlife.

When he had arrived in Tanganda his goal was to photograph the Big Five animals. So far he had snapped three of them: cheetah, lion, and rhino. Mwalimu had promised to introduce him to an elephant herd; that would be number four. He was still lacking the Cape buffalo. As they walked the trail he scanned the plains looking for them.

To the left of the trail was a large herd of impala, flanked by a smaller herd of zebras. Three giraffes sauntered by, headed in the direction of the valley. To the right, five ostriches (a male, two females and two juveniles) trotted purposefully in single file. Such an abundance of wildlife, with many species commingling and coexisting in one place, was common in the Masara Masai. Mwalimu retrieved the Salesman from the real jungle and plunged him back into the Business Jungle with a question that caught him off balance.

"Are you a passionate man, Mwanfunzi?"

"That's kind of a personal question, isn't it? I mean, we haven't even had our first date and you want to know if I'm a passionate man?" he replied in jest, while he wondered what she was talking about.

"Oh, please! Get your mind out of the gutter! I don't mean that kind of passion; I mean are you passionate about your job?"

"I knew that! Am I passionate about my job, huh? To be honest with you..."

Mwalimu interrupted, "Don't be honest with *me*, Mwanfunzi, be honest with *yourself.*"

"Okay, okay. The answer is no. At least right now, I feel no passion for what I do. I used to feel differently; I used to have the fire and passion of an evangelist. But over the last year, the spark has kind of fizzled."

"I thought as much, and it doesn't really surprise me. Often when businesspeople are feeling stumped by the challenges of their businesses, part of the problem is a lack of passion. Without passion there is not the will to persevere in the face of challenge. It's a very common scenario.

"The lessons you've learned so far and the laws that go with them can be followed by doing things that are mechanical: buy advertising, write a business plan, assess your I&A and so on. Regrettably, there is nothing you can do to mechanically rekindle your passion. Passion is a state of mind. To rekindle it you need to adjust your attitude."

"All right, I can buy that," agreed the Salesman. "But how do I do it?"

"I'd like to tell you a story as we walk..."

Among Mwalimu's people it is customary for males in their late teens to become warriors. One of the rites of passage to move from being an adolescent to being a warrior is to participate in the Lion Dance. The dance unfolds as a group of young warriors, armed only with spears, short swords and shields, venture out onto the plains looking for a lion to antagonize. The manner in which the lion is treated is very important. It is meant to test the courage of the young warrior recruits. By the end of the Lion Dance, one lucky recruit will earn a special, highly coveted honor.

Using the tracking skills they have been taught during their training, the recruits will locate a lion. Quickly and quietly they will encircle the lion with their shields held out in front of them. Noiselessly they must close the circle smaller and smaller lest the lion run off through one of the gaps in the circle. When the circle is small enough, the warrior recruits are standing shoulder to shoulder with their shields in front of them, and there is no way for the lion to escape through the shield-wall except by breaking through the circle.

With the circle complete the dance begins. The initiates will dance in place using specific steps and chants that have been used for hundreds of years designed for two purposes. First, they work themselves into a pulse-pounding frenzy. Second, they frighten the lion into fleeing in panic by charging through their circle. Passions rise. The pace of the dance quickens. Chants are screamed at the trapped lion. Tension and suspense rises. Finally the lion bolts.

The young warriors hold their ground; they keep their ranks closed. There are no gaps in the circle; the lion has nowhere to go. They watch the lion closely as they dance and chant, wondering where the lion will ultimately decide to charge through them. *Who will be the lucky recruit?*

Finally the panicked lion picks its spot. Who knows why? The lion has picked one recruit to charge through in its break for freedom. The recruit braces for the impact, raises his shield higher and takes the full force of the collision. As he falls backwards and rolls on the ground, the lion leaps over him and sprints away to safety. The young warrior leaps to his feet, whooping and hollering. His companions surround him with excited congratulations. He was the lucky one. He withstood the lion's charge, and he has won a coveted honor. He will be allowed to wear the revered headdress made from a lion's mane as a testament to his bravery. The lion's mane headdress is a status symbol without peer; every young warrior desires it, but only one member of each class of recruits will earn it.

It might appear that the honor is earned through good luck rather than any other skill or trait. The point at which the lion breaks through the circle can only be a purely random selection, or perhaps not.

Mwalimu's people believe that the lion will be attracted to the spot in the circle occupied by the most passionate recruit; the recruit that has attained the most frenzied state of readiness, who chants the loudest and dances the fastest. Earning the right to wear the lion's mane has nothing to do with random luck. It has everything to do with achieving a passionate state of mind.

"That's another amazing story!" exclaimed the Salesman. "When I was that age I just wanted to survive high school. I thought *that* was hard enough as a rite of passage. Your kids go out and deliberately confront a lion. More than that, they provoke it! Unbelievable! So what do they do to achieve this passionate state of mind?"

"The recruits are given extensive training by the senior warriors and the elders of my tribe. There's a lot of physical training, of course, but just as important—some of the elders think it's more important—is the mental training.

"When we train the warrior recruits to prepare them for the Lion Dance, we help them to understand the grand and noble purpose of the dance. Once they understand the noble purpose, we teach them to stay focused on that purpose. This mind-set helps them to build and maintain a passionate attitude."

"Whoa, wait a minute. You just lost me," the Salesman broke in.

Mwalimu was always very patient with him when he asked intelligent, relevant questions. The Salesman didn't hesitate to ask questions because he knew she wouldn't demean him. It's the sign of a good teacher.

"Okay, no problem. This is an interesting but abstract concept and I want to be sure you get it, Mwanfunzi. Let me describe it another way." She paused briefly to reconsider how to verbalize the concept.

"Remaining focused on the fundamental reason for the thing they are doing makes it easier for the recruits to be passionate. When they think in this manner they elevate that which they are doing from the ordinary to the sublime.

"An example will help to clarify this concept. On a very mundane level, the Lion Dance is nothing more than a complicated series of steps accompanied by a long chant that's older than the hills. If you focus on the Lion Dance at this level it is difficult, if not impossible, to build passion for it. Are you following me, Mwanfunzi?"

"So far so good."

"To elevate the Lion Dance above the mundane we teach the recruits its exalted and noble purpose. That purpose is this: The Lion Dance is the opportunity to earn a grand award that will speak of your great courage to everyone in all of the tribes and bring honor to you and your family for the rest of your life.

"When the Lion Dance is considered from the standpoint of this fundamentally noble purpose it becomes so much more than merely a series of steps and chants that are hard to memorize. From the lofty level of the noble purpose it is easy to maintain and build *passion* for the Lion Dance."

Mwalimu let her words sink in for a moment and then asked the Salesman, "Did that help? Do you get this concept?"

"Absolutely I get it! Basically, what you're saying is that your *attitude* determines your *altitude*. Getting stuck in the mundane traps you at ground level. Focusing on the essential worth of your profession, the 'noble purpose' you called it, will let you soar."

"I think you did get it, Mwanfunzi, but let's make sure. Tell me this, how will this help you rekindle your passion for your profession?"

The Salesman reflected on his work. At its most mundane level all he did was sell stocks and bonds. He'd been in the investment business for so long that he'd sold lots and lots of stocks and bonds. At ground level it was hard to be passionate about *just another day of selling stocks and bonds.*

The noble purpose of his work was quite different. Briefly stated, it was to help his customers achieve their dreams of financial security: to make it possible for a mother to feel the pride of watching her daughter receive her college diploma because carefully selected investments paid for the tuition and all the other expenses; to make it possible for a couple to retire five years early and take the cruise they had dreamed of for years because their investments paid enough dividends and interest to let them afford it. This was his noble purpose: to help customers achieve their financial dreams.

"When I think of my job in those terms I am damn proud of what I do for a living, and it's very easy to get excited about it. When I'm excited, the spark of my passion leaps into a flame again. Thank you for helping me to see that."

"*Your attitude determines your altitude.* You said it yourself, Mwanfunzi."

The Salesman basked in the warm light of his new sense of purpose, his new sense of *passion*. This was why he got into the investment business, and he would carry that passion home with him.

Inevitably his thoughts turned to other people who worked in other businesses. Wouldn't it be wonderful if they could all find and retain a passion for their life's work? It wouldn't be hard; they just had to find the noble purposes that underlay their enterprises. Almost unconsciously, he began considering how the warrior recruits' training for the Lion Dance would apply in the Business Jungle.

He considered a simple paint store. At the ground level of the mundane, the purpose of a paint store is to sell cans of paint, mix the colors, give advice about proper application techniques and so on. When the paint store is viewed from the highest level and its noble purpose is grasped, its mission takes on an entirely new dimension: to help customers turn a building into a home. The paint store becomes a vendor of pride of ownership, an emporium of comfort and coziness. Imagine this: A young couple brings home their first child to the nursery that they lovingly decorated with their own hands using the paint and advice from the paint store. When the coworkers in the paint store can visualize this scene they will know their noble purpose, and they will never again look at a can of paint in the same way.

"You know what Mwalimu? It doesn't matter what you do for a job. Every job has its own noble and exalted purpose. Every person needs to find that purpose, make it their passion, then make it their life's work."

Business Jungle Survival Tool:

A four-step strategy to find the noble purpose of your work

Step 1: Think about the paint store mentioned in this chapter. Now, think about the business you're in. Write about the ground-level view of your business by making a list of the things you do each day. Use a legal pad or a flip-chart.

Step 2: Next, look down on your business from 50,000 feet. What is the fundamental, noble purpose that lies behind the ground-level things you do every day. Write down your noble purpose; it should be no more than three or four sentences.

Step 3: Imagine how your customers will feel when your noble purpose is fulfilled and you have solved the customer's need. Write a short description of what you think these feelings would be. (Think about the story in this chapter of the young parents with their first child.)

Step 4: Imagine how you will feel after you help your customer and fulfill your noble purpose. Write down your feelings.

The Laws of the Business Jungle

20. Use the best equipment.
If the competition has better equipment, they have outgunned you and will start poaching your customers.

21. Rekindle your *passion!*
Find the noble purpose that underlays your job, make it your passion, then make it your life's work.

Chapter Twelve

JUST LIKE COWS

The Salesman stumbled over a rock the size of a brick and realized that the level plains had become rumpled and rocky. He looked ahead on the trail and saw that they would be crossing a series of low humps and mounds. The undulating terrain was strewn with large boulders and covered with thick leafy bushes. The abrupt change in the landscape marked a fault line in the earth, a reminder of the seismic and volcanic forces that shaped this area. These fault lines spread across the landscape like gigantic geologic spider webs, anchored in the north by Mt. Tanganda and in the south by Mt. Kilimanjaro.

About 100 meters ahead the trail passed between a clump of boulders and a thicket of bushes and then curved to the right out of their sight. When Mwalimu reached this part of the trail she stopped and gestured for the Salesman to stand close to her. In a low voice she said, "Do you remember that yesterday, as we were watching the hippos in the river, I told you how dangerous they were?"

The Salesman replied, "Oh, yes, how could I forget? You said that only one animal killed more people in Taganda than hippos."

"Please lower your voice, Mwanfunzi."

"Okay, but why are we whispering?"

"Because yesterday I also told you that there was only one animal I feared more than the hippo." She leaned to her left and looked up the trail as if she were trying to see around the corner.

"What are you trying to say Mwalimu?" asked the Salesman with a growing sense of unease.

"I think it's likely that the animal the native people, myself included, fear the most is close by. Maybe just beyond that curve. It would be wise for us to walk slowly and silently until we see what's around the bend. Stay close to me and try not to say anything, but if you have to speak, please whisper. The last thing we want to do is startle one of these creatures because we risk an attack."

"How can you be so sure that it might be around here?" he whispered.

"Not it, they. This animal lives in a herd. I believe they are nearby because I've seen them in this area before and because they like the broken ground and heavy brush. But the real reason I'm so sure is because we've been following fresh tracks for the last half-kilometer or so."

She turned to resume walking down the trail, but the Salesman grabbed her arm. "Before we go tell me what we're looking for."

"Cape buffalo."

As they reached the curve Mwalimu stopped and listened for a full 30 seconds and then moved slowly forward. Because of the bend in the trail and the thick brush they could see no more than 20 feet of the trail at a time.

A sudden sound of snapping and cracking twigs came from their left. Mwalimu froze. The Salesman stared wide-eyed. Something big was moving through the vegetation but their eyes couldn't penetrate the tangled thicket to see what it was. The Salesman started to speak but Mwalimu shook her head and raised a finger to her lips warning him to be silent.

While they remained rooted to the trail, not daring to move, the invisible animal moved away from them, its path marked by the rustling of branches, snapping of twigs, and the annoyed squawks of birds disturbed in their roosting places. Mwalimu relaxed and leaned over to the Salesman to whisper, "That was a Cape buffalo. We must be careful, but it's safe to continue on our way."

Soon the bend in the trail began to straighten and widen, and the brush was not as dense.

"There," Mwalimu pointed. "Now you can see the Cape buffalo for yourself. We're lucky to see them; they prefer to be in the brush. This is another one of your Big Five game animals, take your picture while you can."

About 50 Cape buffalo were meandering through the clumps of brush and around the scattered boulders. As he focused his telephoto lens on a pair of them, he was struck by their appearance: They looked just like cows. They were happily chewing their cud or grazing on the grass and bushes. But the remarkable thing was their massive horns.

"Mwalimu, there must be something I don't understand. They look just like cows. I'll grant you that they have the biggest rack of horns I've ever seen on a cow, but they still look just like a cow. I was born in the city and raised in the suburbs, but even I know that cows aren't very dangerous. *These* are the animals everyone around here is so fearful of?"

"That's right Mwanfunzi, and the fear is warranted. I think we're far enough away from the herd that we're probably in no danger. By the way, you were right when you said there's something you don't understand about them; actually there are many things. But that's why we're here, so you can observe and learn from them. Before I tell you more about them let's just quietly observe them for a while. It would be a good idea not to make any sudden movements or noises."

A nearby flat-topped rock provided a convenient bench from which to watch the herd. The Cape buffalo does resemble a cow, albeit a big cow. It stands nearly four feet tall at the shoulder and weighs almost a ton. Their most outstanding features are their great horns which span up to five feet from tip to tip. The male's horns are linked by a bonelike structure that covers the front of its head like a massive helmet.

Watching the herd from their boulder/bench the Salesman observed that the Cape buffalo really doesn't do very much. They mostly lie around in the shade and chew their cud or wander lazily as they graze. Occasionally one would flop on its back and wallow in the dust. He was mildly entertained by watching the Oxpecker birds who perched on their backs and hopped all over their bodies searching for insects and parasites on the Buffalo's skin.

He was about to complain of his growing boredom, but when he turned to Mwalimu he held his tongue. She was intently scanning the herd in front of them and even glancing over her shoulder to look behind them. She was not quite tense, but she was extremely wary. Rather than say anything he continued to observe the herd trying to find something interesting or educational to occupy his mind. In the next ten minutes the only thing that happened was that several of the nearby buffalo finally noticed their presence. This happened when the Salesman shifted his weight and his backpack fell off his lap. When the backpack thumped as it hit the ground the buffalo heard it. They abruptly stopped grazing, jerked their heads upright and stared at the two interlopers. Mwalimu stiffened, her wariness elevated to tension.

After fifteen seconds, which seemed like fifteen minutes, the buffalo reached a consensus that Mwalimu and the Salesman were not worth worrying about and returned to their grazing. Mwalimu relaxed into her state of wary watchfulness, and the Salesman realized he had been holding his breath.

Another ten minutes passed and the Salesman could no longer conceal his boredom. Watching the Cape buffalo was hardly more exciting than watching a herd of dairy cows in a Wisconsin pasture. He whispered into Mwalimu's ear asking if they could please be moving on. Mwalimu nodded in agreement. Slowly and quietly they left their rocky bench and resumed walking. Mwalimu never took her eyes off the herd and paid particularly close attention to the group that earlier had stared them down. Luckily there were no buffalo on or near the trail so they were able to stick to it and walk unimpeded. When they finally passed the buffalo on the outermost fringes of the herd Mwalimu actually walked backwards for quite a distance so that she constantly had the animals in her sight. Occasionally her eyes would dart away from the herd for an instant as she looked for things the Salesman could not see.

After the herd was out of sight Mwalimu stopped several times to carefully listen, as if listening for telltale signs of a surprise attack from the rear. She had resumed walking forward but often glanced behind them and continually scouted both sides of the trail. She said nothing so the Salesman remained quiet, too. The tumbled, broken ground and heavy brush gave way once again to the flat, open, oatgrass covered plains.

The Salesman watched Mwalimu as they walked. The farther away from the herd they went the more relaxed she became. When they resumed walking at a normal pace, Mwalimu broke the silence.

"We are well out of the danger zone now. I'm glad I can stop looking over my shoulder so much," she said with a look of relief on her face.

"Wow, those buffalo really had you spooked. I've never seen you so tense."

"Where those animals are concerned, one needs to pay constant attention to the entire herd as well as individuals which could be a threat. I was also continuously assessing escape routes to defensible positions in the event of an attack."

"Oh, so that's it. I was wondering what you were doing those times when you took your eyes off the herd. But, c'mon now, were we really in danger from those cows with the big horns?"

"You don't know how much you've underestimated those cows, Mwanfunzi, but it's perfectly understandable that you have. As a matter of fact, I fully expected this to happen. From what you observed the Cape buffalo appear to be docile, grazing animals that pose no more threat than Daisy Mae, the farm cow. You've not had the opportunity to do any research about this enigmatic creature. I'm going to tell you about the behavior of the Cape buffalo and I think you'll find out that it is a Jekyll-and-Hyde on four hooves. I have a lot to tell you, but it's all germane to this lesson. Please listen carefully."

As they continued forward on the trail Mwalimu explained that buffalo have very little intelligence. Perhaps if they were more intelligent they would be less dangerous. They don't have enough intelligence to be able to feel fear. Consequently there is no animal they fear, and they do not fear man. This sets them apart from every other animal in Tanganda.

Even more sobering is the buffalo's active dislike for humans. They have been known to stalk and kill people who have not threatened them. A buffalo can quickly kill a human by slashing or impaling a person with its horns that are almost as wide as a person is tall, or by crushing and trampling a person using its strength, weight and sharp hooves. People have been known to survive attacks by lions, but no one is known to have survived an attack from a Cape buffalo. Everyone who is in a position to offer an expert opinion on African wildlife agrees: There is no more terrifying a sight than that of a Cape buffalo charging to an attack, head down, horns thrust forward, bellowing in rage, running at 35 miles an hour over or through all obstacles to kill its victim.

"All you have to remember is one thing, Mwanfunzi," Mwalimu concluded. "If a Cape buffalo attacks you, you're a dead man. Simple."

The Salesman had been dumbfounded when he learned about the vicious behavior of the hippos. Now he was overwhelmed by the staggering scope of his misunderstanding about the Cape buffalo's murderous disposition. His chagrin about misunderstanding the buffalo was replaced by a dawning realization of the danger they had faced when they encountered the herd and sat on a rock watching them.

"Mwalimu, we could've been killed back there! You should've told me, should've warned me. I had no idea what I was getting into!"

"Mwanfunzi, every time you get out of bed you could put yourself into a potentially fatal situation. Life is full of risk. If I had warned you, you probably wouldn't have let me take you to see the buffalo and you would have missed this experience."

"Yeah, well what good is the experience if you don't live to tell about it?"

"The reality is that you did live to tell about it. When people ask you about this experience, what will you tell them? Other than being blindsided by me, I mean. What did you learn?" she asked.

"I'm still shaking from the reality of what I just did, and you want me to philosophize about it? I don't think so," he shot back.

"All right! All right! I'm sorry about the way I handled it, but you're being a bit melodramatic."

They walked on in silence. The Salesman sulked; Mwalimu was perturbed. A kilometer passed beneath their sandaled feet when Mwalimu stopped.

"I really am sorry. I didn't have the right to put you into a potentially dangerous situation without telling you first. My motive, even though it may have been misguided, was to give you an extraordinary lesson. I apologize."

The Salesman shrugged. "I know you had the right motive. Maybe I did overreact. Let's just forget this whole disagreement and move on to something more positive."

Mwalimu's smile was incandescent. "Now there's the Mwanfunzi I like best. Come here and give Mwalimu a hug, and the whole thing is forgotten." After a friendly hug, their spirits were revived and they pushed ahead on the trail.

"Here's a positive thing, Mwanfunzi. There is a very good lesson in all this. Would you like to discuss it?"

"Sure. It's getting late in the day and I want to squeeze as much as I can out of the rest of this safari."

"Good. Let's begin. This is a lesson about misunderstanding and underestimating."

When the Salesman first observed the Cape buffalo he did not perceive them to be a threat. He could see *what they looked like* but had no inkling about *what they were capable of doing.* What he saw reminded him of a cow and he incorrectly assumed that the buffalo were an unlikely threat because cows were not a threat. His assumption and his conclusion were 180-degrees off the mark because he formed his opinion in a knowledge vacuum.

This knowledge vacuum was created because he did not have the benefit of doing any research into the behavior of the animal before he formed his opinion. Once the knowledge vacuum was filled by Mwalimu's startling revelations, the Salesman was able to accurately gauge the level of threat that was posed by the Cape buffalo.

In the jungles and plains of Tanganda it is a fatal mistake to misunderstand or underestimate animal behavior. The best way, then, to form an accurate understanding is to combine factual research with field observation. By using this combined approach it's possible to accumulate and interpret all the information needed to arrive at a complete and credible understanding. It's the only way to assess a potential threat.

What does all this have to do with the Business Jungle? Everything.

In the Business Jungle threats from competitors are encountered every single day. Some threats come from obvious sources, but some competitive threats come from unlikely sources. Ten years ago Barnes & Noble, the giant retail bookseller, never dreamed it would be competing against Amazon.com, a virtual bookseller without a single retail outlet. To be a long-term survivor in the Business Jungle, a businessperson must be able to correctly understand the threats posed by all potential competitors. One of the fastest ways to become a victim of the Business Jungle is to underestimate a competitor. It would be foolish to turn your back on the most dangerous animal in the Business Jungle because you thought it was "just a cow."

The same method used to understand animal behavior is the best way to understand your competitors: factual research and field observation.

Factual research means reading about a competitor. Sources of material are virtually unlimited; they include annual reports, ads, brochures, catalogs, news releases and so on. It also means talking to the competitors' customers and asking them what they like and dislike about those competitors. It won't hurt to talk to the competitor herself. When competitors talk to each other they both benefit. Don't expect to learn any trade secrets or proprietary information, but it can be invaluable to learn about competitors from their point of view.

Field research means doing business with a competitor. Bankers need to open checking accounts at other banks. Employees of cell phone companies should obtain cellular service from another cell phone company. Printers should have things printed by other printers. If a competitor sponsors a seminar, be part of the audience. If they open a new store, attend the grand opening or have a secret shopper do it and give you a report.

The desired outcome of this factual and field research is to assign an accurate "threat factor" to each potential competitor. Those competitors that have a low or zero threat factor can be ignored but not forgotten. As time passes, their threat factor could increase, so it's necessary to reevaluate them regularly.

Competitors who pose a high threat will merit close surveillance. To avoid being surprised by the terror of a Cape buffalo's headlong attack, survivors in the Business Jungle need to know their competitor's products and services as well as they know their own. They must know all of the details about features and benefits, costs, the manufacturing process and product reliability.

Once the details are known they should be entered on a competitive analysis spreadsheet. In one column of the spreadsheet, the details of the businessperson's product or service are listed. In the next column, details of the competitor's product or service are listed. Then a side-by-side comparison can be done noting the strengths and weaknesses in each column.

The completed spreadsheet is a highly practical tool. It summarizes factual and field research at a glance and substantiates the threat factor assigned to a particular competitor. It can be used as a resource to "sell against" the competing product or service. It can also be used to facilitate new product design or to help redesign existing products to enhance competitive position.

As he experienced each new lesson, it had become the Salesman's habit to thoroughly consider how each one could be adapted to become a new law of the Business Jungle. When he felt that he understood the lesson and the law, then he would describe his insights to Mwalimu. He followed this pattern for the lesson of the Cape buffalo. He had just finished explaining what he had learned from the buffalo and was summarizing.

"So, Mwalimu, here's the way I see it. The 'what' of this lesson is the importance of understanding my competitors and thereby understanding how much of a threat they may be. The 'why' is because if I have a knowledge vacuum I might overlook a serious threat that could damage or destroy my business. When I'm in the Business Jungle I don't want to repeat what happened out here with the Cape buffalo; I don't want to be yelling at somebody demanding to know why they didn't warn me of the danger. I'll make my own assessment of the danger in advance!"

Mwalimu nodded a little sheepishly. The Salesman continued. "The 'how' of the lesson is to do field research and factual research on each competitor and place the information on a spreadsheet. This is the best way to assign a threat factor.

"Even though I was upset when I found out you had put me at risk when we walked though the herd of Cape buffalo, I guess I'm glad that you did. I learned that I should never enter the real jungle or the Business Jungle if I have a knowledge vacuum. It would be inexcusably foolhardy to ignore the most dangerous animal in my jungle or yours because I thought it was just like a cow."

Business Jungle Survival Tool:

Competitive Analysis Spreadsheet

Your Company	Competitor A	Strengths/Weaknesses	Threat Rating
The Super Widget	**Mega-Widget**		
left & right hand	right hand only	+	0
chrome finish	chrome finish	N/A	0
$1.10 each	$1.00 each	-	8
18-month guarantee	12-month guarantee	+	0
8 sizes	6 sizes	+	0

Overall Threat Factor: 8
(Threat factor scale 1 – 10: 1 = no threat, 10 = highest immediate threat)

1. In the left column, list the features of your company's product. In the middle column, list the features of your competitor's product. In the right column, enter a "+" if your product feature has an advantage over the competitor's. If the competitor has the advantage, enter a "–." Next, assess the threat factor for each feature by assigning a rating between 1 and 10 in the last column. Finally, assess an overall threat factor.

2. Use a similar spreadsheet and evaluation process to compare the benefits of your product to those of the competitor's. Finally, use the spreadsheet to compare the feelings (see chapter thirteen) of the products.

The Laws of the Business Jungle

22. Don't underestimate competitors.

Remember that competition can come from unlikely sources. Do not turn your back on them. Perform careful factual and field research on each competitor. Plot the information on a competitive analysis spreadsheet and assign an accurate threat factor.

Chapter Thirteen

Introducing Njogu

The Salesman wrinkled his nose in disgust. "Ughh! What is that awful smell?"

"I said I would introduce you to an elephant herd, and it would appear that we are getting close to them. What you smell is the aroma of fresh elephant droppings. That big pile over there is the output of a single elephant."

The Salesman looked at the place Mwalimu had indicated and saw a mound two feet high and four feet wide.

"That's the biggest pile of animal poop I've ever seen or ever *want* to see!" he marveled.

"It's the biggest pile you ever *will* see because the elephant is the largest animal that walks the earth today." Mwalimu added, "I'm going to tell you more about the elephants before we encounter them. They are not as dangerous as the Cape buffalo—however, any animal can become dangerous in the right circumstances. The sheer size of the elephant demands our respect and our caution."

"I appreciate your consideration in telling me before we see them instead of after," said the Salesman gratefully.

Mwalimu resumed her overview of elephants and their behavior. "As you know, many native people refer to the lion as *Simba*. Similarly, many natives refer to the elephant as *Njogu*.

"Njogu has a special place among all the animals in the Masara Masai, and it is revered by the native people. It is a magnificent creature not only for its physical size and strength but because it has one of the most complex societies in the animal world and behaves in wondrously profound ways. Somehow Simba has been given the title king of beasts. I believe the title is misapplied because Njogu is the true monarch of the wild kingdom."

Mwalimu went on to describe the gigantic physical characteristics of the bush elephants of the Masara Masai. On average the elephants stand 10 to 13 feet high at the shoulder, which makes the tops of their heads 15 or more feet above the ground. They weigh between 14,000 and 16,000 pounds and are able to eat 500 pounds of food every day.

"Now I understand why those piles were so enormous; that much food input is sure going to generate a bunch of output!" joked the Salesman. "Elephants must be the major fertilizer producers around here..."

The distant trumpeting of an elephant interrupted him. A moment later, an answering trumpet was heard. The call of the wild elephant is the ultimate sound of Africa. It gave the Salesman goose bumps. He had heard many sounds over the past few days, but this was the most awe-inspiring. The roar of the lion was impressive, but it was filled with malice in its primal savagery; it was a sound to fear. The elephant's trumpeting soared majestically across the plains; it resounded with a noble wildness. It was a sound to embrace, a sound to inspire the listener.

Mwalimu interpreted what they had just heard, "That was a mother calling to her calf and then the calf replied."

Elephant society is matriarchal. A single female leads the herd for life, which can be up to 60 years. When the matriarch dies her eldest daughter ascends to the leadership role. This succession of leadership is a behavior that is remarkable in its uniqueness. The herd is made up of a number of clans. Each clan is organized around sets of females, their calves and their elder daughters. Mothers expel young males from the clans as soon as they are able to sustain themselves independently. They will live their lives on the periphery of the herd, either alone or in small groups with other bulls.

Affection is the chief characteristic of elephant society. The animals seem to genuinely care about each other and to form emotional attachments. Not a surprising characteristic considering it is a matriarchal society. Mwalimu related a well-known story of an ecologist who was observing elephants in the field and witnessed a heart-wrenching scene. A member of the herd he was following was sick and dying of old age. The old female staggered, slumped to her knees and then fell to the ground and rolled onto her side. One of her daughters lay her tusks against her and tried to gently help her mother back to her feet, but her mother was too weak to stand. With her trunk the daughter tore a clump of grass from the ground and placed it near her mother's mouth but her mother was too weak to eat. With nothing else to do the daughter stood by her mother gently caressing her with her trunk. A short while later the mother gave a final shuddering breath and died.

The daughter raised her trunk and trumpeted an anguished wail. At the call, the members of the herd came to visit the body. For hours they filed by as if they were in a funeral line. With their trunks they softly touched the old lady in a final farewell. When the last elephant of the herd had passed by, the daughter remained alone with her mother as if she were on watch. From far off she heard the call of the herd's matriarch beckoning her to rejoin the herd. The daughter trumpeted in return, touched her mother's body for the last time and trudged away.

When Mwalimu had finished the poignant story the Salesman felt a lump in his throat. "I had no idea," he said. "Isn't it amazing that the largest land animal is also capable of such tenderness? Amazing."

His eyes had been riveted on Mwalimu while she related the tale. Now he returned his eyes to the trail, but in his peripheral vision he noticed movement. He looked over his left shoulder and stopped in mid-stride. The movement he had seen was actually the bulk of a she-elephant. Mwalimu moved quietly beside him and spoke to the elephant in a hushed reverent tone.

"Greetings Njogu. I would like to present to you this man who is a mwanfunzi; he is my student. It is our hope that you will allow him to learn from you."

Then she turned to the Salesman and quietly suggested that he take a closer look around them, but she cautioned, "In the presence of these animals we should show our respect by speaking softly and moving slowly. There is no danger here for us, but we don't want to startle or unintentionally provoke them."

The Salesman slowly bent his gaze to his left and right and then turned to look behind. From every direction out of the bush emerged a dozen or more elephants and four or five calves of various sizes. His eyes grew round and wide with awe.

"Mwanfunzi, I introduce you to Njogu."

The elephants encircled them. Mwalimu and the Salesman stood at the center of the circle. The elephants were obviously aware of the people in their midst but they went about their grazing and browsing unconcerned. Occasionally one elephant or another would stare curiously at them, flap its huge ears and then return to grazing. The Salesman removed the camera from his neck and snapped four or five pictures. "I almost feel like I should ask permission to take their pictures," he whispered.

"Whether you asked or not, they have given you permission. If they didn't want you taking their picture you would have known!

"This is one of the clans that make up a larger herd. The female I spoke to is the head of this clan, and she is also the matriarch of the herd. She's seen at least 50 rainy seasons."

"You don't really believe she understands you when you talk to her, do you?" inquired the Salesman as he snapped a picture of the matriarch.

"She doesn't understand me in the way you and I understand each other, but I do believe that on some level which we cannot comprehend, she does have some kind of understanding."

The Salesman was skeptical. "That sounds a bit far-fetched to me. But if any animal were able to understand us, I'm sure the elephants would be the first to do it."

While Mwalimu and the Salesman were softly talking, the matriarch had been regarding them with her expressive and intelligent eyes while her ears slowly waved back and forth in the distinctive flapping motion the Salesman had noticed earlier. It almost seemed as if she were intentionally overhearing their conversation. Now there was a pause in the conversation that the matriarch decided to fill by demonstrating to the Salesman that his skepticism was misplaced and that Mwalimu's belief was justified. The regal grandé dame of the herd lifted her head and let forth an ear-splitting trumpet followed by a series of growls, snorts, roars, grunts and squeals.

The song was taken up by nearby elephants and made its way around the circle like a wave. Soon Mwalimu and the Salesman were surrounded by the song, an overpowering wild sonata played by the mightiest instrument in Africa. The wall of sound was thrilling and magnificent. It was so rich that it was almost tangible, and the Salesman could feel it wash over him, leaving a tingling sensation behind. As much as the sound was rich, it was also complex, as complex as any sound produced by the hundred instruments of man in a symphony orchestra. The complexity of the song was due to the astounding variety of noises the elephants could produce.

While the song was being played the Salesman turned 360 degrees as he watched and listened to the elephants. When he turned back to his original position Mwalimu was alongside him and they both faced the matriarch. The Salesman's body reverberated with the echoes of the song. Then, as suddenly as it began, the song abruptly ended.

Mwalimu had a faint smile on her lips as she observed his reaction. Then she said to the matriarch in the same reverent tone, "*Asante*, Njogu. I will help this Mwanfunzi to appreciate the lesson you have offered. I wish you safe travel."

Mwalimu and the matriarch regarded each other for a moment. The Salesman thought he saw a look of mutual respect pass between them but dismissed it as imaginary. Then the matriarch bellowed to her clan, turned and lumbered off into the bush. The circle of elephants unwound as the clan followed their leader westward into the lowering sun. In less than 20 seconds the entire clan had melted into the wild landscape. For a few minutes they could be herd plowing through the vegetation as branches cracked and snapped with their passing, and then there was silence.

The Salesman shook his head and blinked his eyes as if he were emerging from a day dream, and at that instant there came a distant trumpeting.

"That's Njogu saying goodbye to us," she interpreted once again, looking in the direction of the sound.

"Mwalimu, I'm not sure what just happened here. Whatever it was, it's one of the most spiritual experiences I've had."

"Yes, Njogu was generous to us today. I think we should talk about what really did happen just now. The elephant choir eloquently demonstrated their varied communication styles. It was an honor for us to hear them; very few people have heard what we heard. There are lessons here and more laws to be written for the Business Jungle."

The teacher and the student turned south to complete the final segment of their safari. To their right the sun continued its inevitable descent. Insects chattered. A gentle breeze was just strong enough to disturb the branches of an acacia tree and send a flock of grackles airborne. Thoughts of the elephant encounter preoccupied them both.

At length the Salesman said, "You know, I think that the she-elephant was trying to prove something to me. Maybe you were right, maybe she did somehow comprehend what you said. It almost seemed like she was listening when you asked her to allow me to learn from her. Then she led the clan in that wonderful song as if that was what she wanted me to learn. Am I being crazy?"

"No, you're not being crazy. You were part of an extraordinary event, and you're having a little trouble understanding it. Let me help you figure out what it means."

Mwalimu explained that the matriarch had offered lessons on several different levels. The surface level lessons had to do with the elephant's ability to communicate by using oral and aural techniques that are unique among land animals. Biological studies have shown that elephants are able to make at least 15 distinct audible sounds. They use this repertoire as an elephantine vocabulary to warn each other of predators, locate wayward calves or to keep track of each other as they roam the plains. Perhaps this is what the matriarch wanted the Salesman to know and was the reason she led her clan in song.

In addition to this extensive audible vocabulary, elephants also communicate across distances of several miles using infrasound (sounds that are out of the range of human hearing). The elephants' huge ears and listening abilities allow them to hear these infrasound messages which man will never hear. Mwalimu noted that this combination of oral and aural communication tools are unique to the elephants.

Drilling down to a deeper level, she said that these lessons about the manner of communication between elephants had relevance to the Business Jungle. They are particularly relevant to the sales process.

The sales process, as Mwalimu described it, had three undeniable truths. First, the *sales* process is in reality a *communication* process. Second, the only viable sales process is one that is based upon the prospect's needs, or "needs-based." Third, maximum results can only be achieved when *transactions* are replaced by *relationships*.

In order to sell goods or services, businesspeople must communicate with their prospects. The role of the businessperson within this communication process is to be a facilitator—that is, to keep the process moving forward, to control its direction and listen a lot while only talking a little. She was adamant about this point.

The Salesman interrupted. "Excuse me, Mwalimu. What you're saying sounds logical, but I'm not sure how realistic it is. You say that the businessperson should listen but not talk very much. In my business, for instance, I need to gather a lot of information and thoroughly discuss a customer's investment objectives. I need to talk a *lot*."

"That's an interesting comment, thank you. However I disagree with your conclusion that you need to talk a lot. From something you said yesterday I don't think you really believe it anyway," Mwalimu responded.

"What did I say?"

"Yesterday morning shortly after we left my *vijiji* we had our first encounter with the wildlife. It was with the zebra herd, remember?" she recounted. "As we watched the zebras you were telling me how you would gather information from customers and prospects so that you wouldn't be confused by their stripes."

The Salesman recollected the interlude, "Yes, I do remember. I told you that I needed to ask questions that would encourage a person to tell me what they wanted to accomplish."

"Exactly!" exclaimed Mwalimu. "One of the keys to this communication process is to ask the right questions. If you can become a skilled inquirer you won't have to talk much. You simply make the appropriate inquiries and then listen closely while the customer answers with the information you seek. This technique of inquiring is also a way to control the direction of a conversation and to keep it moving forward if it should start to lag or stray from the main point. Does that make sense?"

"It makes perfect sense," he agreed. "Instead of talking I just need to ask simple, pointed questions and then sit back and listen."

"That's it and it sounds to me like you're already using this process, at least some of the time."

"Yes, I do it some of the time but I really need to do it all the time, don't I?" The Salesman knew the answer to his question even as he asked it.

Mwalimu acknowledged that it was a hard habit to learn. "It's not an easy behavior for humans to learn. We want to dominate conversations; we love to talk about ourselves. But in the Business Jungle businesspeople should listen 80% of the time and only talk 20%."

"I've noticed that you're a very good listener, Mwalimu. I feel like I want to tell you things. How do I become a good listener?"

"Let me answer your questions by posing another question to you. What have you noticed about my listening skills that makes you feel that you want to talk to me?"

The Salesman's mind returned to a conversation he had with Mwalimu about the cheetah and the gazelle fawn. He recollected how well Mwalimu had listened to him. But what was it about her that made her listen so well?

First, she gave him her complete attention. She looked him directly in the eye almost constantly. She didn't do anything else but listen. She didn't fiddle with her clothes, she didn't walk around, and she didn't in any way appear preoccupied by anything

Business Jungle Survival Skill:

A three-step strategy for active listening

Step 1: Focus your complete attention on the speaker.

Step 2: Use appropriate body language.

Step 3: Repeat or rephrase what the speaker says.

except what he said to her.

Second, she used appropriate body language—smiling at amusing comments, nodding or shaking her head at appropriate times and leaning toward him as a sign of her active interest and involvement in listening to him.

Third, she let him know that she was truly hearing and comprehending what he said by periodically repeating back to him the things he had just told her.

When he told Mwalimu about his observations of her listening skills she replied that active listening was a simple but exhausting discipline. It is far more mentally tiring to listen than it is to speak. However it is worth the effort because by following those simple listening techniques, the customer or prospect will want to tell the businessperson everything about her situation and that makes the businessperson's job a lot easier.

Then Mwalimu advised the Salesman, "Remember the elephants' huge ears and their unique listening ability and maybe it will remind you to listen to your customers and prospects."

At this suggestion the Salesman hoped that the photos of the elephants would come out well. With these pictures he had achieved his goal of capturing the Big Five on film. Beyond that, he wanted to stand a small picture of an elephant on a corner of his desk as a constant reminder to listen.

A pair of tall flame trees arched over the trail ahead. The light breeze that prevailed sighed through the branches and sent a small shower of the brilliant red-orange cup-shaped flowers floating down around them. As they passed into the rainfall of petals Mwalimu resumed her discourse on the sales communication process. She reminded him of her earlier assertion that the only viable sales process is one that is needs based. Businesspeople who fail to understand this truth are doomed in the Business Jungle. Just as those who try to close a sale by browbeating or intimidating a prospect will become extinct, so too will businesspeople who fail to use a needs-based approach to selling.

The logic behind needs-based selling is as simple as it is compelling. Consumers go shopping for a product or service because they have a problem (a need) and they want help solving it. What's more, customers and prospects often have multiple needs making it necessary for the businessperson to find out what the person needs *most* and then proposing a solution. In summary then, the businessperson must identify what the prospect needs most, propose a solution, and then conclusively demonstrate why the proposed solution will work to solve the prospect's need. If the needs-based approach is correctly applied, the prospect *will almost always buy* the product or service that is proposed because it is the solution to meet their need.

The opposite of needs-based selling is product-based selling. The former provides a product or service that fits the prospect. The latter tries to fit the prospect to the product. Product-based selling focuses on what the business wants to sell, rather than on what the prospect wants to buy. This approach to selling is a disastrous strategical and tactical error because it can only provide short-term results. Consumers might be convinced to buy the product or service, but when they discover that it doesn't solve their problem, they will never be repeat customers. They will never provide a referral; instead they will probably tell their associates that they were treated badly.

Long-term survival in the Business Jungle depends on maintaining the goodwill of the consumers. Providing meaningful solutions to people's problems earns goodwill and assures the flow of repeat business and referrals.

"I told you the story of the dying elephant and her daughter for two reasons," said Mwalimu. "One reason was to illustrate how elephants seem to form emotional attachments with each other. In other words, elephants have relationships. The other reason I told the story was to use it as a reminder of the importance of relationships in the sales/communication process."

Many businesses and businesspeople today practice transaction selling instead of relationship selling. They operate under the misguided belief that the number of transactions that are processed determines sales success. Such businesspeople attempt to complete each transaction as rapidly as possible and then move on to the next. They only talk to the prospect long enough to get the briefest hint about what the prospect is looking for, show the prospect a product and close the sale. Transaction selling permits no time for building rapport with the prospect or for after-the-sale follow-up. The object is to limit the time spent with the prospect so that the next transaction can take place.

Like product-based selling, transaction selling is a big mistake. Not surprisingly, businesses that utilize transaction selling are also often product-based sellers. These businesses may enjoy short-term success in the Business Jungle, maybe even spectacular short-term success, but it is unlikely that they will become long-term survivors. Certainly if they can produce a high enough volume of transactions they can increase their lifespan, but sheer volume does not guarantee survival. Transaction sellers fail to grasp the meaning of the elephants' lesson about relationships. Businesspeople would be well advised not to form *emotional attachments* with their customers and prospects. However, forming *relationships* will produce more business over a longer period of time.

Relationship selling is the antithesis of transaction selling because it requires the investment of time by the businessperson. It is not surprising then that relationship sellers often use a needs-based sales approach. Once the relationship is solidly built its lifetime is measured in terms of years rather than as a single transaction. Relationship selling often precludes the possibility of the immediate gratification provided by transaction selling; short-lived gratification is shunned in favor of long-term results. Cultivation and relationship selling are similar because they both require time and patience, but the eventual harvest will provide plenty of sustenance.

Establishing a relationship takes extra time because rapport must be developed with the prospect, careful inquiry must be made about the prospect's needs, a thorough explanation must be provided about the product or service that is proposed, and after the sale has been completed, careful follow-up must be scrupulously maintained. Relationship sellers willingly exert the effort and invest the time to do all of these things because their goal is long-term survival and prosperity in the Business Jungle.

Mwalimu summarized by saying, "Businesspeople who break this law of the Business Jungle by remaining product-based transaction sellers do so at their own peril, for it may put them on the endangered species list."

The Salesman added, "Yep, and they'll be there on the list right next to the hard closers and the businesspeople who deny that they are also salespeople. Their days are numbered!"

The Laws of the Business Jungle

23. The sales process is a communication process.
Within this communication process the businessperson's role is to be a facilitator and a listener.

24. The only viable sales process is one that is "needs-based."
Providing meaningful solutions that meet the needs of customers and prospects will assure the flow of repeat business and referrals.

Chapter Fourteen

N. M. B. R. S.

The sandals Mwalimu had given to the Salesman had molded to his feet and they carried him comfortably along the trail. He and his teacher had walked a long way since their dawn departure from Mwalimu's *vijiji*. Calculating the true measurement of this safari would not be possible simply by counting the kilometers. The true measurement of this safari was in the sum of his experiences, all the observations he had made, all the lessons he had learned, and all the laws of the Business Jungle he had come to appreciate. Now, as he neared the end of the safari, he felt pleasantly tired, both physically and mentally. His body was no longer sore, his breathing came easily and he was just a little bit sunburnt. It felt good to be comfortably weary. He had exercised his mind as much as his body over the past couple of days. His mind was filled with new ideas, a new sense of purpose and self-confidence and the stimulation of his rekindled passion.

Cresting the top of a small rise they saw below them, barely a kilometer away, the circle of Mwalimu's *vijiji*. Mwalimu paused at the top of the crest to gaze upon her home. The afternoon was softly melting into evening. The sun's mellowing rays slanted across the savannah painting the *vijiji* in a golden glow.

The Salesman stood next to his teacher and said, a little wistfully, "We're almost back. I thought we were getting close but I didn't realize we were this close to closing the circle of the safari."

Mwalimu nodded silently.

"I'm not ready to walk into your *vijiji* just yet. Could we sit here for a while and talk? I still have so many questions. And I'm not sure I understand part of the lesson of the elephants."

Mwalimu slowly and gracefully sank to the ground and sat cross-legged facing her *vijiji*.

"Tell me, Mwanfunzi, what is it you don't understand?"

"You see, I think this lesson is very pertinent to my particular part of the Business Jungle. As a stockbroker I am very much a salesperson, but I've been thinking that this lesson may not be universally pertinent throughout the Business Jungle."

A slight frown quickly clouded Mwalimu's usually jovial face. "Oh?" she said. "Please tell me more about this."

The Salesman began, "We agree that every businessperson is also a salesperson."

Mwalimu nodded affirmatively. Encouraged, the Salesman marched ahead. "But I think that there are different degrees of applicability of the sales/communication process. In other words, some businesspeople need to apply the process more than others."

Then the Salesman hit a brick wall. Mwalimu shook her head vehemently. "I disagree entirely. It is my firm belief that every business and every businessperson, without exception, would benefit by thoroughly applying a needs-based selling philosophy. I can understand why you might have your opinion though. Your opinion is shaped by your extensive professional experience in an industry involving sales cycles, where great sales skills are a requirement for success. I think you're rather proud to be a salesperson. I think you're rather proud to be a salesperson and that you're very good at it. I also think that you're somewhat contemptuous of businesspeople who are less skilled than you or who fail to admit that they are a salesperson as well as a businessperson."

Her frown was replaced with her customary grin. "I think that perhaps a slightly broader perspective on this issue is in order. I'll tell you the basis for my opinion and at least you'll have the benefit of another perspective. Maybe I can even convince you that my opinion has some merit."

This is what Mwalimu said, "Every business should adopt a needs-based selling approach. *Every business.* It makes no difference whether the business is a corner grocery store or a multi-national corporation. It makes no difference whether the business sells socks or stocks, silverware or stereos." To prove her point Mwalimu used a shoe store specializing in athletic shoes as an example.

"Most people would agree that not much true selling goes on in a shoe store. What *does* go on are a lot of transactions. A typical shoe store transaction might go something like this:

"An employee says 'Can I help you?' or many times the customer has to get the employee's attention by saying 'I need some help please!' The employee then makes a superficial analysis of the customer's needs that's usually limited to inquiring about shoe size. The customer scans the displays of shoes, attempts to understand the dizzying array of features of the different brands and models, and tries to make some judgments about price versus value. The employee will perhaps point out a certain shoe that is 'featured,' which means that there is a huge number of them in the warehouse. They are sometimes called specials, which means they have a higher profit margin for the store.

"At length the customer makes a selection and the employee disappears into the storeroom to ferret out a pair in the right size. Assuming the employee is successful, the customer tries on the shoes, takes a few tentative steps around the store and finalizes the buying decision. The cashier is paid, the transaction is complete and the customer walks out the door and never hears anything from the shoe store again."

The Salesman had a knowing look on his face and nodded vigorously. "Yep, that's about the way it is in every shoe store I've been in."

"What if," Mwalimu posed, "the shoe store used a needs-based, relationship selling approach? That transaction would unfold in a completely different way, wouldn't it? In fact, it wouldn't be a *trans*action at all—it would be an *inter*action and the beginning of a beautiful relationship, as Humphrey Bogart would say."

If the transaction in the shoe store could be rewound like a videotape and then replayed in a needs-based/relationship-selling mode it would indeed have little resemblance to the first version. In fact, the transaction would have transformed into an interaction in which both the employee and the customer had important roles. The employee morphs into a salesperson and attempts to build rapport with the customer, learn about the customer's situation, understand all of the customer's needs, propose solutions to the needs, and finalize the interaction. There are two very intentional side effects of an interaction conducted in this manner. First, the customer is significantly more likely to make a positive buying decision. Second, the interaction becomes the first brick used in the building of a relationship with the customer.

A closer look at the revised version of the transaction-turned-interaction shows that the customer would be promptly and professionally greeted shortly after entering the store. Then a few moments would be spent establishing rapport as the salesperson introduces himself, welcomes the customer, puts her at ease, and determines the reason for her visit to the store.

Next, the salesperson would begin inquiring about the customer's situation and ultimately uncover her needs. While he is making his inquiries he would be listening closely to the customer's replies because nestled within them will be the customer's needs. Finding these needs is the whole point behind the inquiries because once they are understood the salesperson can propose solutions that meet the needs. As the salesperson puts forth a proposition that will meet the customer's needs he would thoroughly explain the benefits and features of the proposition. For it is only when the customer understands the benefits and agrees that they meet her needs that a positive buying decision will be made.

To finalize the transaction the salesperson summarizes his proposition by reminding the customer of the benefits to which she previously agreed. The salesperson then suggests the next steps that need to be taken and seeks agreement on taking those steps. When such agreement is reached the interaction is complete. Although the interaction is complete, the process is not over. The interaction was merely the first step in building a relationship with the customer.

Time is the prerequisite for relationship building. The construction material includes interactions with the customer, service after an interaction in which a purchase is made, and regular ongoing follow-up. The building process is never complete, although a milestone is achieved when the salesperson securely occupies the top of the customer's mind when she needs to make another purchase or make a referral. In the customer's mind, running shoes should forever be associated with the shoe store in this illustration. For that association to occur the customer must believe that the shoe store has meaningful solutions to her needs and her best interests in mind—that her interests are placed above the interests of the shoe store itself. When the relationship reaches this milestone the customer will return to the shoe store to buy more shoes as she needs them, and she will send her friends to the store, too.

Mwalimu fixed her eyes on the Salesman and asked, "Now, Mwanfunzi, tell me. Which shoe store will do more business over a long period of time? The first store is a product-based transaction seller. It's interested in processing a high volume of transactions quickly and pushing certain products on customers, which serve the best interests of the store. On the other hand, will the second store, which is a needs-based relationship seller, be more prosperous? It learns about the customer's needs and proposes a solution to meet the needs. After the sale occurs, the shoe store strengthens its relationship by staying in touch with the customer. Soon, the shoe store and running shoes are synonymous in the customer's mind.

"Which shoe store would you do business with? Which will be a long-term survivor in the Business Jungle?"

"This is a no-brainer; the second store will be the survivor," answered the Salesman. "The first store might do a lot of business, for a while. Sooner or later customers will stop coming because they were sold a product that didn't really meet their needs or because the word is out that it's a bad place to shop or simply because customers lose interest due to the lack of a relationship."

"I hope now that you have a better understanding of why I feel so strongly about this issue, Mwanfunzi. Every businessperson *does* need to be a salesperson, but they must also specifically be a needs-based relationship seller."

"This time I get to ask you the 'how' question," said the Salesman, and they both grinned. "I appreciate that needs-based relationship selling is a superior approach to the sales-communication process, but I don't understand how to utilize the approach."

"I think you understand more than you realize. For example, you've already told me that you use a certain type of question to obtain information about a customer's needs, so you are already using some of the inquiring techniques I mentioned."

"Yeah, but there's a lot more to it than just asking questions; that's too easy," he said skeptically.

Mwalimu nodded. "Indeed there is more, we could spend another two or three days discussing this topic. But the day is growing short and we need to return to my *vijiji* soon, so I will give you an overview of this fascinating and successful approach to selling. I'll call it Needs-Most Based Relationship Selling, or N.M.B.R.S. for short."

Needs-Most Based Relationship Selling - N . M . B . R . S .[©]

Before looking at the "how" of NMBRS, it would be wise to consider the "why." The "why" can be expressed rather succinctly:

♦ to thoroughly understand the customer's need and propose a relevant solution

♦ to meet those needs and to build upon the solutions to establish a relationship

The "how" of NMBRS is a bit more intricate:

the salesperson must master a series of logical verbal behaviors to control
the direction of the interaction and to achieve the desired outcome.

The desired outcome has two objectives, one short-term and the other long-term. The short-term objective is to reach a mutual agreement with the customer pertaining to the interaction at hand. The long-term objective is to occupy the top of the customer's mind.

NMBRS is not a sales script. It is not a formula, nor is it a sales system. Selling is communicating, and interpersonal communication is too malleable to fit into the rigid structure of a formula, system or script. Besides, good salespeople are too creative and independent to accept the imposition of a formula upon their interactions with customers. NMBRS is a *process* in the true sense of the word—that is, a series of acts aimed at a single end. It is not meant to replace or alter the salesperson's natural communicative talent; rather it is a pathway that a salesperson can follow during an interaction with a customer or a prospect. However, if the series of behaviors that are recommended in the NMBRS process are properly applied, they will provide a pathway whose ultimate, and virtually inevitable, ending is the achievement of both the customer's and the salesperson's desired outcomes.

Many communication behaviors are recommended in the NMBRS process, and these behaviors are elaborately interwoven; they work together as one behavior supports and enhances another. If one behavior is lifted out of the process or used in isolation, the salesperson might still have a pleasant, even fruitful, discussion with the customer but the desired outcome is unlikely to be achieved. But if the process is left intact then the salesperson will walk with the customer down an ever-narrowing path using the NMBRS behaviors as signposts to stay on track and moving surely closer to the destination. Reaching the destination and achieving the desired outcome is almost assured.

For the past three days the Salesman had been on a safari of self-discovery as he trekked across the vast savannah. As he listened to his wise mentor and seemingly tireless safari guide, he was beginning to appreciate that NMBRS is a safari too—a verbal safari. He remembered that Mwalimu had once advised him that every safari begins with a single footprint in the dust, but no safari is ever completed until all the succeeding footprints have left their marks on the trail. So it is with NMBRS.

The verbal behaviors flow in a logical manner from the very start of an interaction, which is like taking the first footprint in the dust of the trail outside the village to begin a real safari, to the very end of the process when the desired outcome is achieved, which is similar to the eventual arrival at the journey's end. Throughout the verbal safari the NMBRS behaviors can act as signposts pointing toward the journey's end. The salesperson can confidently follow the signposts regardless of the twists and turns the interaction might take and know that he will always be able to find his way to the destination.

The Salesman told Mwalimu that he considered NMBRS to be a verbal safari. She was intrigued by the concept and agreed that it was a fitting analogy.

"Let's take a verbal safari right now, Mwanfunzi. I'll explain each of the NMBRS behaviors and then apply them to the interaction in our shoe store. Are you ready to depart?" she asked.

The Salesman ground his foot into the dirt leaving a distinct footprint.

"Ready!" he said. "And I've made the first footprint!"

The equivalent of the first footprint in NMBRS is called "the welcoming." It consists of three verbal behaviors:

    1. The Greeting   2. Building Rapport   3. Getting Serious

Successfully completing these behaviors is crucial because they set the tone for the rest of the interaction. For the same reason that the front door of a business should be clean and attractive because it's the first thing the customer sees, so should the beginning of an interaction be well presented; it will provide a good entrance for the interaction. Let's look at each of the three behaviors of the welcoming more closely.

The Welcoming

1. The Greeting

The purpose of the greeting is to make the customer feel welcome and open to the possibility of doing business.

When a customer or prospect walks into a place of business she should be greeted promptly; good business sense and common courtesy demand it. If the customer is arriving as the result of a pre-scheduled appointment then the greeting should be immediate. If the customer arrives without an appointment, such as walking into a retail store, then the greeting doesn't need to be immediate; in fact it probably should *not* be immediate. This is because the customer may feel that she's being pounced on, and such a feeling puts most people on the defensive. Putting the customer on the defensive is not the way to begin an interaction and is the opposite of the original intention of the greeting. Allowing the customer to look around for a few minutes before being greeted is a friendlier approach.

The mechanics of the greeting are uncomplicated. The customer is welcomed, the salesperson introduces himself and shakes hands with the customer, and he determines why the customer has come in. Granted, in some businesses (automobile repair shops come to mind) it's impractical to shake hands. Nevertheless, the salesperson should always give his name. In most cases the customer will respond by giving her own name. Use her name often; the sweetest sound anyone can ever hear is the sound of her own name.

2. Building Rapport

Customers do business with people they trust. Customers trust people with whom they have rapport. Salespeople need to build rapport with customers. Each of the three verbal behaviors contained in the welcoming help to build rapport in one degree or another. Indeed, each and every one of the behaviors contained in NMBRS helps to build rapport. During the early stages of an interaction it's especially important to begin building rapport and, by extension, to begin building trust.

Rapport building is the process of establishing connections with the customer that are separate from the business at hand. It is the process of connecting with the customer on a human level rather than on a strictly business level. It communicates to customers that they are appreciated as people not merely as business transactions.

This process must be done with sincerity. The salesperson must be genuinely interested in learning about the customer. If the process is attempted insincerely it will fail miserably. Customers can detect phoniness in a nanosecond. If the salesperson attempts to subvert the rapport building process by turning it into a short cut to make a sale, then the customer will recognize what's happening and throw up the defenses. If the salesperson has no interest in learning about the humanity of the customer, then not only will NMBRS fail but the salesperson is in the wrong business and needs to find something else to do for a living.

Perhaps the best way to build rapport is to find something in common with the customer. When common ground has been found it becomes easier to relate to the customer on a personal level and it's easier for the customer to relate to the salesperson. The common ground also becomes a place from which rapport can be built in other ways.

3. Getting Serious

At some point in the early stages of the interaction it will be time to get serious and get down to business. After all, the customer walked in for some reason and probably wants to accomplish something. The point at which it is time to get serious becomes self-evident. Either the customer will indicate that she's ready to get down to business or there will be a natural pause in the rapport building where the salesperson can steer the interaction toward more serious topics.

This verbal behavior in getting serious entails reaching an agreement with the customer about a to-do list for what's going to happen during the rest of the interaction. It's most advantageous for the salesperson to propose this to-do list because it will establish his leadership role in the interaction. Staking a claim to the leadership role will allow the salesperson to control the flow of the interaction. The customer will generally yield to the salesperson's leadership if she is confident that the salesperson is keeping her needs foremost; the list must be based upon the customer's agenda, not the salesperson's agenda. Assuming the role of leader early in the interaction will help keep the interaction on track later.

When the salesperson proposes the to-do list he must also demonstrate why this particular to-do list will be of value to the customer. If the customer doesn't see any value in spending her time in the manner proposed she won't agree to the list and the interaction will grind to a halt. The salesperson is going to have to revise the to-do list until the customer agrees to it and then the interaction can proceed.

Reality Checks

Throughout any interaction the salesperson should frequently be seeking small agreements with the customer. These agreements are called "reality checks." Usually the first reality check occurs after the salesperson has proposed the to-do list, although they should be sprinkled liberally all through the interaction. The purpose of the reality checks is to make sure that both the salesperson and the customer are comfortable with what has been said and are ready to move on.

They usually take the form of simple, confirming questions. For example:

◆How does that sound?

◆Do you have any questions?

◆Is there anything you want to add?

◆Are you ready to move ahead?

Inquiring

Assuming that the customer and the salesperson have agreed on their to-do list it's time to move on to a more substantive part of the interaction in which the salesperson asks about the customer's situation. This verbal behavior is called "inquiring." Its purpose is to ask appropriate questions in order to discover the customer's needs. Discovering these needs is something like peeling another one of those little wild onions. To understand the customer's needs the salesperson needs to peel away the outer layers of the customer's situation. Peeling off the outermost layer requires that the salesperson ignore his suppositions about the customer's needs so that he can see the customer's true situation. It is only human nature to think we know what a customer wants, but that is a supposition and it may not be correct. The salesperson must discard all the suppositions he brings to an interaction and let them be replaced by the facts of the true situation.

Full and complete understanding of the true situation comes from further peeling of a couple more layers of the situation onion. This is done by inquiring about the customer's "dispositions" and "conditions." Under these two layers is where the salesperson is likely to finally discover the customer's needs, but yet another layer must be peeled away to reach the center of the situation onion. This final layer is removed by sorting through the customer's needs, prioritizing them and ultimately discovering that which the client "needs most." This is the center of the situation onion.

The most effective method in which to inquire is to use a combination of "encouraging inquiries," which encourage the customer to talk openly about her situation, and "confirming inquiries," which are used to confirm the salesperson's understanding of the customer's situation or to obtain specific pieces of information.

Encouraging Inquiries

Encouraging inquiries are broad and general in scope and nature. They invite and encourage the customer to respond at length. For example:

- ♦ Tell me about your running schedule.
- ♦ What do you like about running?
- ♦ Describe the perfect running shoe.
- ♦ What do you like about your current pair of running shoes?

Confirming Inquiries

Confirming inquiries are very narrow and specific in order to elicit succinct responses that provide detailed information or confirm the salesperson's understanding of what has been said. For example:

- ♦ How many miles do you run each week?
- ♦ What is your running pace?
- ♦ How long does a pair of running shoes normally last?
- ♦ Do you have a price range in mind?
- ♦ Did I hear you say that you run mostly on dirt trails?

Often the two types of inquiries are used in tandem. Usually a confirming inquiry is made first, and then depending on the response, it is followed up with an encouraging inquiry. For example:

Salesperson: Have you had any recent running injuries? *(confirming inquiry)*

Customer: Yes, as a matter of fact, I have.

Salesperson: Please tell me about them. *(encouraging inquiry)*

Supposition vs. Situation

Salespeople sometimes make the mistake of thinking they know what the customer wants and needs. They make assumptions about the way people behave, and out of these assumptions spring generalizations that are applied to customers. The end result is a "supposition" about a specific customer. The obvious risk is that the supposition doesn't apply to the individual standing in front of the salesperson at any given time. If the supposition is in fact faulty then the entire interaction is jeopardized because the salesperson has little hope of ever learning the customer's true needs.

How much success will a salesperson have if he supposes that the customer in front of him wants to run *faster*, when the customer's true need is to run *farther*?

In reality every customer is different. The only way a salesperson can find out about the customer is to ask her. The verbal behaviors used in inquiring allow the customer to tell the salesperson exactly what her true situation is. The salesperson no longer has any need to assume, generalize or suppose and can proceed unhindered to the center of the onion. Along the way the salesperson must learn about the customers "dispositions" and "conditions."

Dispositions

The way a customer feels about her situation and the way she envisions her future situation are called "dispositions" and "conditions."

Dispositions are the stuff of dreams, desires and emotions. The importance of knowing and appreciating these dispositions cannot be overstated. Why? Because making a purchase decision is an emotional decision, not a logical one.

Here is one of the great truths of the sales communication process:

A person does NOT buy something because of what it *does* for them;
they buy it because of the way they imagine it will make them *feel*.

A customer does NOT buy a pair of running shoes because they are lightweight or because they have a jelly-filled pocket in the heelcup or because they have really cool colors and graphics. A customer buys them because she imagines how it will feel to have those new shoes carry her farther and faster with greater comfort while she enjoys the admiring glances of the people who notice her flashy footwear.

Since the first salespeople were trained, they were coached to sell features and benefits. That wisdom is outdated and has been transformed through several stages of evolution into a new wisdom. This new wisdom has reached its highest stage of evolution in NMBRS.

At first salespeople were taught the feature/benefit technique: For every feature the salesperson must explain at least one benefit. Then insightful salespeople began to realize that customers considered benefits more important than features, so the technique evolved into benefit/feature. The emphasis was now on

Business Jungle Survival Skill:

For every benefit, the salesperson must help the customer imagine how she will *feel* because of the benefit.

selling the benefit and ignoring the feature unless the customer asked about it. The next evolution came when salespeople realized that buying decisions were emotional, not logical, and that the buying decision depended only on the benefits. Once again the technique evolved, this time into benefit/benefit.

Even the more enlightened benefit/benefit technique does not fully encompass the great truth of selling: People buy something so they can feel a certain way. The highest stage of evolution of the technique is benefits/feelings. The new wisdom of NMBRS is that *for every benefit, the salesperson must help the customer imagine how she will feel because of*

the benefit. Unless the salesperson understands the customer's dispositions it is simply not possible to use the benefits/feelings technique.

To ask a customer about her dispositions, the salesperson uses an encouraging inquiry, which focuses like a laser on her feelings and emotions. For example:

♦How does it make you feel when you set a personal best record in your favorite race?
♦How does it make you feel when someone says, "Wow, you must be in great shape?"
♦How does it make you feel when you perform beneath your capability?

Conditions

The customer's current state of being is called "conditions"; they are the facts and figures of the customer's situation. As much as dispositions are abstract, conditions are specific, logical and rational. While few purchasing decisions are ever made solely because of a customer's conditions, it is likely that they will have an effect on the purchasing decision. For this reason it is necessary for the salesperson to know them. Knowing the conditions is especially helpful when the salesperson gets to the point of proposing solutions to the customer.

Another way to think of conditions is that they represent where the customer is now, while dispositions represent where the customer wants to be in the future. If the salesperson can propose a solution to bridge this gap then the customer will make a positive buying decision.

To learn about the customer's conditions the salesperson will generally use confirming inquiries because he's searching for specific pieces of information. For example:

♦What size do you wear?

♦What brand of running shoes do you have now?

♦Do you need to buy a new pair of shoes today?

♦Do you have a price range in mind?

These sample inquiries illustrate the utility of knowing a customer's condition. A salesperson doesn't want to show the customer a pair of shoes costing $149 if her budget is $75.

The Laws of the Business Jungle

25. Benefits/Feelings

For every benefit, the salesperson must help the customer imagine how she will feel because of the benefit.

Chapter Fifteen

PUTTING N.M.B.R.S. TO WORK

So far in the NMBRS process all of the effort has been aimed at uncovering and understanding the customer's needs. Until the needs are understood, no solutions can be proposed. Until the solutions are proposed, no buying decisions can be made. Until the buying decisions are made, no business can be transacted.

Needs Most

It is during the process of inquiring that the needs will be unearthed, but the salesperson will need to be alert and attentive to the verbal and nonverbal cues that signal the needs.

The most obvious cue is when the customer says: "What I need is...," or "What I'd really like to do is...," or "Here's what I want...," or something similar. When the customer uses this kind of language it's like seeing a great big red EXIT sign in a dark room—there is no doubt about what it means. The customer has signaled a need because she has expressed a desire to do something that will improve her current conditions and also honor her dispositions. When the salesperson hears such a cue he should pounce on it immediately because this is the point at which the selling in Needs-Most Based Relationship Selling begins. This part of NMBRS includes two verbal behaviors: completing a "needs inventory" and determining "priority of needs."

1. Needs Inventory

"Pouncing on a need" means using a confirming inquiry to verify what was just said by the customer and using encouraging inquiries to obtain a full understanding of the need.

When the salesperson is certain that a need has been expressed and that he fully understands it, he must note the need on a "needs inventory." The inventory can be listed physically on a note pad or it can be listed mentally in the salesperson's mind. The choice of method is immaterial. What is material is that the salesperson keep careful track of each need because once they are uncovered they are precious and not to be wasted. The needs inventory serves two purposes. First, most customers have more than one need but all needs must be known before they can be prioritized. Second, each need offers to the salesperson an opportunity to propose a solution that can result in additional new business after the primary need is solved.

2. Priority of Needs

When the salesperson is satisfied that he has uncovered and understands all of the customer's needs he must now find out the primary need, that which the customer "needs most." The best way to zero in on the primary need is to review with the customer each of the needs on the needs inventory and prioritize them in terms of their importance to the customer and the customer's timeline. Generally the most important need and/or the need that requires the fastest solution will be what the customer "needs most."

Using a confirming inquiry will help establish the primary need. For example: "Which is more important to you, lightweight running shoes or running shoes with a lot of cushioning? When do you need them? Is it more important for you to have the shoes today or if I don't have the right color, do you want me to order them?"

When the primary need has been identified and understood then the first proposition to solve the need can be made.

Propositions

An objective of NMBRS is to position the salesperson as a problem-solver. The manner in which this positioning takes place is by the use of a verbal behavior wherein the salesperson proposes a meaningful solution for what the customer needs most. These are called "propositions." When the proposition is accepted by the customer, implemented and subsequently solves the customer's needs, then the salesperson becomes a problem-solver. Viewed in this light the salesperson is elevated to the role of valued ally whom the customer can rely on for solutions. In this role it is likely that the salesperson will receive additional business from the customer and the likelihood of receiving referrals is also enhanced.

Propositions must be presented properly. The first proposition must propose a solution to what the customer needs most. The proposition must not only solve a need, but it must be tailored to fit the customer's dispositions and conditions or the customer simply won't accept it. It will be necessary for the salesperson to help the customer understand how the proposition meets her needs by painting a vivid picture about how she will feel when her need is met. In some cases it may also be necessary to explain the features of the product or service contained within the proposition. There are three steps in this verbal behavior:

1. Restate the primary need from the needs inventory.
2. Explain the benefits/feelings of the proposition.
3. Do a reality check.

Eventually the salesperson will propose solutions to each of the customer's needs, but the most important thing is to offer a proposition to solve the primary need first. That's because the customer is more likely to make a quick buying decision when it pertains to solving what she needs most—meaning that a transaction will occur faster. Keep in mind that if the salesperson starts proposing solutions to secondary needs he runs the risk of appearing to ignore the customer's agenda in favor of his own. When the primary need has been solved, the foundation of a relationship has been built. The salesperson has been successfully promoted to the role of problem-solver and he will have the luxury of taking additional time to follow up with the customer for the purpose of discussing every other need on the needs inventory. The proposed solutions to the remaining items form the basis of the cross-selling/up-selling activities that will take place at the appropriate times in the future.

The salesperson must strive single-mindedly to achieve an agreement with the customer that the proposition will meet her dispositions. When the customer can visualize how she will feel when the salesperson's proposal has been implemented and when she believes those feelings honor her dispositions, then she will make a positive buying decision. There is no other decision she can make. The interaction is nearly complete. In the real world of the Business Jungle the road from the primary need to an accepted proposition is not always smooth. A variety of issues can arise that prevent the customer from making a positive buying decision. These issues are called "roadblocks."

Roadblocks

A roadblock is a barrier that prevents the customer from making a positive buying decision. Usually roadblocks are encountered because the customer simply needs more information. The salesperson must figure out a way to go over, under, around or through a roadblock in order to clear the way for the customer to make her decision. There are five types of roadblocks and they can be overcome by providing specific kinds of additional information to the customer:

1. Waiters
2. Stoppers
3. Bloopers
4. Doubters
5. Yawners

1. Waiters

Waiters are customers who can't or won't make a decision. They wait for their need to somehow magically resolve itself. Waiters usually delay their decision because they have too much information and can't understand it, in which case the salesperson must interpret the information for them. Conversely, waiters may delay their decision because they have too little information and feel that they are in the dark, in which case the salesperson must determine exactly what kind of specific information they need to make a fully informed decision. Waiters fail to grasp the urgency of their situation, in which case the salesperson must create a sense of urgency for them.

2. Stoppers

Customers who want something the salesperson can't provide are called stoppers. It's an apt name because if the salesperson can't provide a solution, then the sales communication process is stopped. In this situation the salesperson may be able to propose a partial solution; it just may not be exactly what the customer was expecting. If the customer wants hiking boots but the store only sells running shoes, then there's nothing that can be done. However, if the customer wants brown hiking boots but the store only carries black hiking boots, the salesperson can knock down the obstacle. The salesperson can do this by reminding the customer of all the things the black hiking boots can do which will solve some, most or all of the customer's needs. Then the salesperson must help the prospect understand that these reasons outweigh the issue of color selection.

3. Bloopers

A blooper occurs when either the salesperson or the customer makes a mistake or when a miscommunication occurs. Simply correcting the mistake easily knocks down this roadblock. For example, the customer thinks that the shoe store only carries running shoes when in fact it also carries hiking boots; the salesperson gives the correct information and points to the display of hiking boots.

4. Doubters

These customers doubt that something the salesperson has said is really true. Doubters don't think the salesperson is dishonest or telling a lie—they are simply skeptics. Usually a doubter needs to be convinced that the salesperson's statements are true by seeing hard data from a third party. When they see the verifying information that comes from what they consider to be a credible source they will accept the salesperson's proposition.

5. Yawners

Yawners are complacent. Either they don't believe they have a need or they believe the need they have is unimportant and doesn't need to be solved. Yawners are different than waiters because waiters recognize that they have an important need. To knock down this roadblock the salesperson must make the yawner realize that a need exists and why it is important to solve it in a timely way.

Subsequent to knocking down any roadblocks, or if propositions were immediately accepted, the salesperson begins the final dash to conclude the interaction. This is called reaching agreement.

Agreement

The objective of the agreement is simply to concur on what the next steps in the interaction will be and when they will take place. In some cases the next step is for the customer to actually make her purchase. In other cases there may be intermediate steps that must be taken before the customer finalizes her buying decision. In either case the agreement is successful as long as there is a meeting of the minds about what the next steps will be and when they will occur. Here's a highly effective way to structure the agreement:

1. Summarize the primary need and the proposition that meets the need.
2. Remind the customer of her previous agreement that the proposition would meet her need.
3. Remind the customer of the way she will feel after the proposition is implemented.
4. Propose a specific set of next steps.
5. Make a reality check.

Business Jungle Survival Skill:

N. M. B. R. S.:
Needs-Most Based Relationship Selling

- The Welcoming
    - ♦ The Greeting
    - ♦ Building Rapport
    - ♦ Getting Serious
- Reality Checks
    - ♦ Inquiring
    - ♦ Encouraging Inquiries
    - ♦ Confirming Inquiries
- Dispositions and Conditions
    - ♦ Needs Most
    - ♦ Needs Inventory
    - ♦ Priority of Needs
- Propositions
    - ♦ Roadblocks
- Agreement

Mwalimu smiled at the Salesman and placed a weathered hand on his shoulder. "With the successful completion of the agreement the interaction is complete, but the relationship building has just begun. Like so many of the laws of the real jungle and like many of the other laws of the Business Jungle, NMBRS is a great circle. As the relationship grows and blossoms the opportunity will arise for more business with the customer, then the NMBRS process begins over again. Recognizing and understanding these great circles and harnessing their power can help assure longevity in the Business Jungle."

The Salesman remained silent for a moment as his mind finished absorbing and processing the enormous amount of information Mwalimu had just given him.

As if she was reading his mind, she patted his shoulder and said, "I know I've just presented you with a lot of new information and I can almost hear the wheels of your mind turning as you consider it all. Now you can understand why I said that we could easily spend a couple of days talking about this."

"Yes," he replied. "I do understand and you did dump a lot of data on me just now. However, as I was listening I recognized bits and pieces of it as behaviors I'm already doing. I'm sure that I'm not doing the entire process, but sometimes I do parts of it."

"I know you are Mwanfunzi. Your skills will be even better when you use all of the verbal behaviors all of the time. The NMBRS process that I've just described is a method that will help you organize your communication so that it will be more effective."

"You know what they say, Mwalimu, *practice makes perfect.* I have an idea. Let's do a quick role-play; you be the customer and I'll be the salesperson in the shoe store. I'd like to see how it feels to use the NMBRS process in a sales interaction."

"Great idea!" beamed Mwalimu. "It'll be fun; let's do it."

Salesperson: Hi, welcome to the store. I noticed that you walked in a few minutes ago and I wanted to introduce myself. My name is Troy. What brings you into the store today?
(*NMBRS verbal behavior*: the greeting)

Customer: Oh, hi. My name's Kate. I work near here and when I was walking by I remembered that my running shoes are starting to wear out.

SP: I'm glad you came in Kate. I see you're wearing a t-shirt from the New Year's Day 10-K Run. I ran in that myself. Wasn't that a great band they had playing at the finish line? (*They chat for a minute about the run.*)

(*NMBRS verbal behavior*: building rapport)

C: I don't have much time right now, so I need to look at some shoes.

SP: OK, I appreciate that you're on a tight schedule. Here's what I propose we do: I need to ask you some questions about your running and what you're looking for in a pair of shoes, then I can show you some shoes that will meet your needs. That way you can make the most of the limited time you have to spend here today. Does that sound okay to you?

(*NMBRS verbal behavior*: getting serious)

C: That'll be fine.

SP: Tell me, Kate, what do you like most about running?

(*NMBRS verbal behavior*: encouraging inquiry about dispositions)

C: I like the way I feel after I'm done. You know what I mean? It's a good kind of tiredness. I guess I also like the fact that I'm keeping myself in good shape.

SP: Yes, I know what you mean about the good kind of tired. How many miles do you run each week?

(*NMBRS verbal behavior*: confirming inquiry about conditions)

C: I run about 30 miles a week—5 days a week, 6 miles each day.

SP: On what kind of surface do you run?

(*NMBRS verbal behavior*: confirming inquiry about conditions)

C: Mostly on dirt trails at County Park.

SP: So, Kate, it sounds like you've got a busy running schedule —5 days a week, 30 miles a week and all on trails. Is that right?
(*NMBRS verbal behavior*: confirming inquiry to verify information)

C: That's right.

SP: What would be the perfect pair of running shoes for you?
(*NMBRS verbal behavior*: encouraging inquiry about dispositions)

C: I need a pair of shoes that has a lot of cushioning. I would like it to have a sole that will grip the trail so I won't slip and they need to be durable and easy to clean.
(*NMBRS verbal behavior*: customer has expressed several needs, which the salesperson needs to note on the needs inventory)

SP: Okay, that's a good list of requirements. Did you have a price range in mind?
(*NMBRS verbal behavior*: confirming inquiry about conditions)

C: I want to spend less than $100.
(*NMBRS verbal behavior*: adding another need to the inventory)

SP: I want to be sure I understand what you need, Kate. You said that you need a shoe that will cushion your foot, has enough tread to keep you from slipping, is durable and easy to clean. You also want to keep the price less than $100. Is that about it?
(*NMBRS verbal behavior*: confirming inquiry to verify needs inventory)

C: Yes, that's what I need.

SP: Is there anything else you need—anything at all?

C: I don't think so.

SP: Which of those things is most important? You mentioned cushioning first; would you say that's what you need most?
(NMBRS verbal behavior: confirming inquiry to determine primary need)

C: Yes, I suppose it is. If I don't have enough cushioning I get a lot of pain in my heel and I have to shorten the run or even stop running.

SP: It's more important than tread design, durability, ease of cleaning, or price?

C: Yes, but I really don't want to spend more than $100.

SP: I get the picture, Kate, and I appreciate the importance of your needs. I propose that you consider the All Terrain Trainer made by the UltraCool Shoe Company. Now I want to tell you about the benefits of owning this shoe. You'll feel hardly any impact when your foot hits the trail because the cushioning is so plush. You'll be practically as sure-footed as a mountain goat so you won't have to worry about falling because of the tread design. Finally, you won't have to worry about exceeding your budget. How does that sound?
(NMBRS verbal behavior: using the benefits/feelings technique to explain the benefits)

C: Sounds pretty good.

SP: Now let's talk about how those benefits will make you feel about your running. Imagine this: You've just completed a really good training run in the park. Your body has been challenged and now you're in better shape than you were yesterday. While you're doing some stretches as you cool down, you suddenly realize that your feet do not hurt and you've just had one of the most comfortable runs you've ever had. That would feel pretty good, right?

(*NMBRS verbal behavior*: using the benefits/feelings technique to explain the feelings the benefits can provide)

C: Yeah, that sounds great.

SP: Let me summarize what we've talked about. Your primary need is a shoe that has lots of cushioning and costs less than $100, has a good tread design for trail running, and will be durable and easy to clean. We discussed a shoe called the All Terrain Trainer, and you agreed that it has all the benefits you're looking for. You were able to imagine how it would feel to run in these shoes, and it felt pretty good.

(*NMBRS verbal behavior*: the agreement—summarizing primary need and proposition)

I suggest that you try these on to make sure they fit properly. When we have you fitted correctly you can buy the shoes today for $89.95 and turn that feeling into reality on your very next run. What do you think?

(*NMBRS verbal behavior*: the agreement—proposing specific next steps)

C: I don't know...they don't look like they will be very durable.

(*NMBRS verbal behavior*: roadblock, customer is a doubter)

SP: That's an excellent point. I'm glad you brought it up. *Stunning Running Magazine* just rated this shoe as one of the most durable all-terrain shoes available. Here's a copy of the article. Does that make you feel better about the shoe's durability?

(*NMBRS verbal behavior*: knocking down the roadblock with third party data)

C: Yes it does. I think I'd like to try them on now. If they fit, I'll take them.

"Well done!" Mwalimu laughed as she slapped the Salesman on the back. "You sold me a pair of shoes!"

"I guess I did, didn't I?! I think you were pretty easy on me though; you only put up one roadblock. Regardless, it felt good to use the verbal behaviors in NMBRS. It seemed very natural. They really did provide signposts to help guide me through the interaction."

"Remember though," Mwalimu said, wagging her finger at him, "at this point you've only completed a trip but not an entire journey. You've gone as far as the NMB part of NMBRS; you successfully completed a Needs-Most Based interaction. What about the RS part, the Relationship Selling?"

The Salesman thought for a moment. He absently stared up at the sky, which was beginning to dim to twilight as the sun fell to the hem of the clouds.

"The successful interaction is the beginning of my relationship with the customer. Just the way I spoke with her using the NMBRS verbal behaviors has allowed us to bond better than we would have otherwise. I think that we're off to a good start."

He thought again and resumed. "To build on this beginning I might call the customer in a couple of weeks to see how the shoes are doing. As time goes by I would send her notices of promotions that she might be interested in. I'd also do friendly stuff. For example, maybe a good race has been scheduled in a nearby park; I'd make sure she was aware of it by sending her the details."

"Those are some very good relationship selling ideas! Nice job, Mwanfunzi!" said Mwalimu, again slapping him on the back. Then more seriously she said, "I hope you realize how rich our elephant encounter has proved to be. From that encounter alone you have discovered many new laws of the Business Jungle. And now we must finish our journey, for the circle of your safari is nearly complete."

Business Jungle
Survival Tool:

A four-step strategy and a NMBRS worksheet you can use to create a great welcoming

There are four verbal behaviors in the welcoming:

1. The Greeting
2. Building Rapport
3. Getting Serious
4. Reality Check

Step 1: The Greeting

Write down what you would say to a prospect who walked into your place of business or to whom you were speaking on the telephone. You want to say something that makes the prospect feel welcome and open to the possibility of doing business with you.

_____

Now, repeat aloud what you've just written—it should take less than 10 seconds. Next, practice it until it seems natural. Finally, role-play with someone to try out your greeting.

Step 2: Building Rapport

Write down two ideas of things you can say to a prospect that will connect with them on a human level. These two ideas can be your all-purpose rapport builders. Don't make this too hard; they can be simple things. For example:
     "How much snow did you get at your house during last night's blizzard?"
     "How about those Packers!?"

Your idea #1 _____

Your idea #2 _____

Repeat them aloud. Practice them. Role-play.

Step 3: Getting Serious

Think about a typical interaction with a prospect. Write down a hypothetical to-do list that you could propose to this prospect during the hypothetical interaction.

To-do List _____

Next, write down a value statement for this to-do list.

Value statement _____

Repeat aloud the to-do list and the value statement. Practice them. Role-play.

Step 4: Reality Check

Write down three ways that you could ask for a small agreement from the prospect regarding the to-do list. For example: "Are you ready to move ahead?"
1. _____
2. _____
3. _____

Read aloud. Practice. Role-play.

Finally, put it all together. Repeat the greeting, then build some rapport, then suggest a to-do list and offer a value statement, and then do the reality check. Now you have a great welcoming!

The Laws of the Business Jungle

26. N. M. B. R. S.[©]

Every business should adopt a Needs-Most Based Relationship Selling philosophy as the most effective way to sell products and services and build relationships.

Chapter Sixteen

HAKUNA MATATA

Mwalimu and the Salesman began the final short segment of the safari that would return them to the starting point from which they had embarked at sunrise the day before. As they made their way down the gently sloping hill where they had been sitting, the Salesman noticed that someone had built a large bonfire to one side of the common area. Villagers would gather there later to socialize, tell stories, hear news from other villages and simply enjoy each other's company. A cloud of dust caught his attention and he saw that the men and boys were converging on the village, returning with the herds of cattle that had been grazing by day on the plains. The cattle would be safely enclosed in the center of the village circle, protected by the thorny fence that repels predators.

The Salesman mused that there was no thorny fence to protect him from the predators in the Business Jungle. His protection was the new knowledge he had gained from the wild, brave, resourceful animals that lived in this incredible place. His personal thorny fence was the lessons the animals had taught him and the laws of the Business Jungle that he had distilled from those lessons.

Teacher and student walked side by side as they approached the entrance to the *vijiji*. About 30 meters from the entrance the Salesman suddenly stopped. He turned to Mwalimu and simply said, "Thank you." Then he offered her his arm and together they re-entered the *vijiji*. They closed the circle of the safari just as the sun fell below the western horizon.

They walked across the *vijiji*'s circle and made for the bonfire. As they walked, many villagers said hello and welcomed them back. The Salesman recognized the mask painter and the sandal maker he had seen the first day he entered the *vijiji*. They pointed and waved to

Mwalimu and the Salesman and when they saw them walking arm in arm, they nodded knowingly to each other and smiled.

"It looks as if Mwalimu has helped another mwanfunzi to find that which he was seeking!" said the sandal maker to the mask painter.

The Salesman caught the sandal maker's eye, lifted one foot, pointed to his sandal and called out "*Asante*!" The sandal maker waved back and returned to her work.

When Mwalimu and the Salesman sat on the ground near the communal bonfire two young girls materialized carrying bowls of steaming beef stew and small gourds filled with beer. Until he smelled the savory stew he hadn't realized how hungry he was. While he gratefully gobbled a large spoonful of stew Mwalimu said that there was one more lesson she wanted to discuss.

"Do you know about the philosophy of *hakuna matata*?" she asked.

The Salesman nodded, his mouth full. He recalled the enlightened way in which problems were viewed using this philosophy.

Mwalimu explained that the mind-set of *hakuna matata* applied to many different kinds of life experiences, but perhaps the most important of its applications had to do with keeping a person's life properly balanced. She and the Salesman had just spent two days immersed in the raw, primal beauty of Tanganda's savannah as they learned new survival skills to help the Salesman prosper in the Business Jungle. Now she cautioned him that the pursuit of prosperity must not become so important as to overshadow other more precious aspects of life. When prosperity becomes a preoccupation (or worse, an obsession) a person's life becomes unbalanced and unhappiness is often the result.

The greatest blessing a person can have is peace of mind. To be free of worries, fears, doubts and confusion, to be at peace with oneself and the world is a state of mind every person ultimately hopes to attain. It is not possible to find peace of mind if a person's life is out of balance.

The Salesman swallowed another mouthful of stew and said, "It sounds like what you're saying is that I shouldn't go overboard with all of this stuff about the Laws of the Business Jungle. If all I do is work then my life's balance is out of whack, right?"

Mwalimu agreed, "That's right Mwanfunzi. And if your life gets too unbalanced because you're working too much, even your working habits will eventually suffer."

"All right then, how do I stay balanced?" he asked.

"To understand the answer you need to understand another important circle. I call it the Circle of Balance."

Mwalimu drew a large circle in the dirt in front of them and divided it into four parts. Each of the four parts represented a necessary component of a well-balanced life. The parts were labeled: work, self, family and community.

The slice of the circle called "work" is self-defining. It's a person's job, her livelihood, how she earns an income. "Self" refers to activities that a person does just for herself, for no other reason than for her own enjoyment. For some people this takes the form of exercise, or gardening, or sleeping late on Sunday morning. "Family" includes time spent with spouse and children, with other family members, or with those who are of significant importance. This time might be spent by taking vacations together, everyone sitting down together at the same time for a meal, reading a bedtime story, attending a soccer game in which a son or daughter is playing, or just talking. The last slice of life in the Circle of Balance is labeled "community." It represents the activities a person undertakes in recognition of the fact that we are all a small part of a greater whole. It includes giving back to the community through community service projects. This slice also includes those things that celebrate the spiritual or religious aspects of life. It is the opposite of self because it embraces the people with whom a person interacts.

A person with a well-balanced circle of life spends time in each part of the circle. She doesn't necessarily spend equal amounts of time in each part because not everyone requires equal portions of the four slices to find peace of mind. Some people may need to spend more time in self, while others need to spend more time in work. Each person's circle will be different, but the only way to balance the circle is to consistently spend time in every part of the circle, enjoying every slice of life.

Once a person discovers what the ideal portions are for each slice of her circle she must strive to keep them in balance. Modern life has a ballistic pace and a relentless lack of predictability which may make it necessary to spend more time on one part of the circle than was ever contemplated. Perhaps a big project comes up at the office, which requires that many more hours than normal be spent in the work slice. On the other hand, perhaps a parent becomes ill and care giving requires an unusual amount of time in the family slice. When this happens, it's okay; these temporary imbalances are an inevitable part of life. Temporary imbalances are okay as long as they are not allowed to become permanent. It becomes important to periodically take stock of one's personal circle, to make judgments about the amounts of time spent in each slice, and to adjust and re-balance as needed.

"You see, Mwanfunzi, we already have all the time there is. No matter how hard we try we can't create any more of it. When we are first put on this earth our individual life-clocks start to run. One of life's greatest unsolvable mysteries is that no one knows how much time we have on that life-clock before it runs down and we run out of time. We only learn how much time is on our life-clock when it's too late to do anything about it."

The Salesman stared into the dancing flames of the bonfire. "I understand what you're saying. It's rather sobering..."

"Yes, but there is some really good, uplifting news, too. We may already have all the time there *is*, but we also have all the time we really *need*. When we live our lives in a balanced way we don't need any more time than what we have. The circle I've shown you here in the firelight is a tool we can use to help us manage and allocate our time so it is well spent."

The fire was reflected on the richly dark and shiny skin of Mwalimu's face. Once again the Salesman noted the serenity in her expression and realized that its source was her attainment of a perfectly balanced life. She had achieved peace of mind.

The Salesman looked into Mwalimu's deep dark eyes. "This is the most important lesson of all, isn't it?" he asked softly.

"Yes, Mwanfunzi, it is."

Four days later the Salesman was back in the middle of the Business Jungle: the desk in his 23rd floor office in a downtown office building. Sitting in the middle of his desk was the backpack Mwalimu had provided for his use during the safari. Before he left her village she had taken the backpack and disappeared into her hut for almost an hour explaining that she needed to prepare something for him. She left him to stare into the fire and reflect on his completed safari. He realized that although his safari was now complete it was only just the beginning of his education about how to survive in the Business Jungle. He knew with certainty that there would be more safaris in his future.

When Mwalimu reappeared she handed him the backpack as a parting gift but she made him promise not to look inside it until he was back in his office. The Salesman had kept his promise and had left the backpack closed since Mwalimu handed it to him. Not even the US Customs Inspector looked into the backpack or asked the Salesman what was in it. He had absolutely no idea what might be contained in the backpack, but he never let it out of his sight and rarely was it out of his hands for the entire trip home. Other travelers watching him might have thought the scruffy backpack was stuffed with rare treasure by the way he watched over it. To the Salesman it didn't matter what was inside, whatever it was it would be something precious to him.

As he reached for the backpack he gazed around his office where he had displayed mementos of his safari. His sandals were placed on the bottom shelf of his bookcase where they were easily accessible. He would find that he would wear them often when he was struggling with difficult business challenges. On the wall directly in front of his desk were his photographs of the Big Five animals of Tanganda. They had turned out to be all that he had hoped for. He had made a collage of all five photos and had them framed in a single large frame made of lustrous ebony. He chose this exotic African wood because it reminded him of Mwalimu's beautiful skin. Perched on a corner of his desk between the telephone and his appointment book was a 3x5 snapshot of Njogu's magnificent head with her expansive ears flared wide.

The Salesman pulled the backpack toward him and untied the cord that cinched it tightly closed. Immediately he detected a familiar aroma. He laughed quietly to himself as his hand closed on something small and round; he knew immediately what it was as he withdrew a small Tangandan wild onion. Staring at the onion in his hand, his mind wandered back to the game trail he had walked on; he remembered how he had wrestled with the warthog's lesson about image and attitude while he unconsciously peeled an onion Mwalimu had given him.

He placed the onion on his desk and reached into the backpack again. This time he felt a small bunch of leafy twigs—it was myrrh. Mwalimu had shown him how to make a toothbrush with this plant at their campsite on the Masara River. The myrrh was placed on the desk next to the onion and he reached into the backpack a third time to remove the last object. He felt that it was round, flat and hard. Puzzled, he pulled it from the backpack and looked at it closely. It was an ebony disc about three or four inches in diameter and half an inch thick. It felt cool and heavy in his hand and its finish was smooth and glossy. He turned the disc over and caught his breath. Deeply inlaid in the ebony was a magnificent Circle of Balance. The circle and its slices of life were inlaid by some kind of silver-gray wood that almost glowed in contrast to the black ebony. Each slice was labeled in the colorful style of the mask painter he saw in the *vijiji*, and the rest of the circle was decorated here and there with the same colorful paint. He would have to find a very special place to display the cherished Circle of Balance.

He lifted the backpack to move it from his desktop but he heard a crinkling noise like paper being wrinkled. Curious, he reached inside but found nothing. Then he remembered the small pocket sewn to the inside of the main compartment that was meant to hold small odds and ends. He slipped his hand into the pocket and found an envelope. When he pulled it out into the light he saw that it was addressed simply as "Mwanfunzi." The letter inside was beautifully handwritten in small, precise letters that almost looked like script. It began "Dear Mwanfunzi," but before he read it he skipped to the bottom to verify that it was really from Mwalimu. Sure enough, there at the end was her signature in the same precise handwriting. The Salesman returned to the top of the page and began to read.

Dear Mwanfunzi,

As I write this I can see you through my doorway sitting and watching the bonfire in my vijiji. *You have just completed your first safari, and judging by the pensive look on your face I feel certain that you have achieved the true purpose of a safari: personal growth and renewal. The first day I met you I said that I doubted you were ready to learn and that you would be a difficult student. Thank you for proving me wrong.*

Throughout our safari together you tried to learn more about me but I refused to tell you anything. It was not important for you to have that knowledge then, but now that the experience has been completed I am ready to answer your questions.

Although I was born in my vijiji *and am content to die here, I spent many years outside of it. I was the first, and only, woman from my* vijiji *to receive a university education. I earned a degree in economics at Oxford in England and my MBA at Wharton in the USA. While I was attending Wharton I became a fan of American football, and the San Francisco 49'ers became my adopted "home team."*

Eventually I returned to England to work for a small food importer. I persuaded the elderly owner to update and expand his existing line of imported food items by adding Tangandan coffee to the line. It proved to be a fortunate decision when he agreed to my suggestion. There was a large demand by British coffee drinkers for coffee from Tanganda and the business grew rapidly. My responsibilities with the company continued to grow. After a few years of continued growth and prosperity the owner retired and moved to Italy. I became the Chief Executive of the company. Once again fortune smiled on me and I presided over the company's continued rapid growth until it became the largest coffee importer in Europe.

During this time I was able to hone my leadership skills with the help and patience of the team of employees with whom I worked. I am the manager who asked her team to review her performance. I became the leader whom people would follow just to see where I would take them. The place we ended up going was the stock exchange, because when the company was judged ready it became a public corporation. By the way, my investment bankers persuaded the General to join my Board of Directors; he served the Board for many years and became a close friend.

Eight years ago, at the so-called height of my success, I realized that I was terribly unhappy. My life was so overwhelmed with my work that my Circle of Balance had only one big slice. I resolved to take a holiday and return to my vijiji; it was my hope to go on a safari, much like you did, to search for clarity of understanding about my unhappiness. During that safari I discovered the Circle of Balance, and I never went back to my job. I have remained here in the vijiji *of my birth, and I have found peace.*

Hakuna matata my friend,
Mwalimu

The Salesman leaned back in his chair and silently shook his head in amazement. He reread the letter twice. Finally he sighed heavily and murmured to himself, "I'll be damned!" He placed the letter on his desktop next to the other things and stood up to look out his window. He stared at the frenzy of the cityscape that spread out before him. As he stood there, fragments of memories of his safari wafted through his thoughts like the breeze that ruffles the tall red oatgrass on the Tangandan savannah.

The harsh buzz of his telephone snapped him back to reality. *The Business Jungle is restless today,* he thought. Then he laughed and reached for the phone.

— End —

The Law of the Business Jungle

27. *Hakuna matata*, my friend.

The Laws of the Business Jungle

- Partnering: Good partnerships make you stronger than you were separately.
- The new Three R's: respect, responsibility and resourcefulness
- Don't be confused by the stripes.
- Increase the herd with advertising.
- Inside each problem is an opportunity waiting to be discovered.
- Have a great plan.
- Be opportunistic.
- Focus and persistence
- When the sun rises you had better be running - *fast*.
- The importance of I&A
- The "when" of I&A
- Define your territory.
- Dominate your market.
- Brush your teeth with myrrh.
- Choose your hunting mode—lion or cheetah.
- Cultivate. Don't stalk.
- Businessperson = Salesperson
- Prune away clients and prospects.
- Care about the people you lead.
- Use the best equipment.
- Rekindle your *passion!*
- Don't underestimate competitors.
- The sales process is a communication process.
- The only viable sales process is one that is needs-based.
- Benefits/feelings
- N. M. B. R. S.
- *Hakuna matata*, my friend.

About the Author

On his 25-year personal safari through the Business Jungle, Tom Brown has always been a successful salesman with a natural flair for marketing. Over the course of his career he has been a banker, stockbroker, financial planner, entrepreneur and corporate leader.

As a banker, he successfully helped banks in California and Nevada transform their stale 10-to-3 bureaucracies into vibrant, aggressive and proactive sales cultures. As a stockbroker with two of the nation's largest brokerage firms, he was a production leader, winning numerous sales contests. As an entrepreneur, he established a financial planning firm that grew to include real estate brokerage, insurance brokerage, mortgage brokerage, estate planning, investment management and financial consulting.

Since his early retirement from the vice-presidency of the nation's full service/reduced commission stock brokerage firm, he has become a sales consultant with many prestigious corporate clients. *Zebras Don't Wear Pinstripes* is the first of five *Business Jungle Books* soon to be released by Cypress Publishing Group. The series includes *The Ears of the Elephant*, *Growing Tusks*, *The Lion Dance* and *The Circle of Balance*.

The Business Jungle
Sales Success Series

You've read the book.
You've taken the first step on your safari into the Business Jungle.
Now what?

Enter*Train*ment! Sales Inspiration Workshops is pleased to offer the Laws of the Business Jungle Sales Success Series. Using the practices and principles found in *Zebras Don't Wear Pinstripes*, the Sales Success Series will help individual salespeople and entire sales organizations to successfully achieve their professional and business development goals.

To discover a list of seminar and workshop themes and other important information call Enter*Train*ment! directly at (916) 638-3243 or visit our website at www.businessjungle.com, then click on the Enter*Train*ment! tab.

presented by

Enter Train **ment !**

Sales **Inspiration** Workshops ®

The Author's donation policy:
*The animals of Africa are of vital importance to the biological diversity of the planet AND to our success as salespeople. The author will donate a portion of the profits from **Zebras** and its ancillary business activities to select nonprofit organizations whose mission is to aid these wonderful animals. These organizations include:*

- *The Africa Wildlife Foundation*
- *The Elephant Research Foundation*
- *The Jane Goodall Institute*